DEBT

DEBT

Slavery in Disguise

How I Paid Off a Debt of Half a Million Dollars in Three and a Half Years

Obioma Anukwuem

To order additional copies of this book, contact:
Xlibris
1-888-795-4274
www.Xlibris.com
Orders@Xlibris.com
740888

CONTENTS

Dedication vii

Preface 1

Chapter 1: Know Who You Are 7

Chapter 2: Do Not Fool Yourself 23

Chapter 3: Change Your Mentality 39

Chapter 4: Recognize You Are in Debt 57

Chapter 5: How We Paid Off Our Debt 73

Chapter 6: Stay Out of Trouble—Be Resolute 89

Chapter 7: Be Content but Do Not Settle 103

Chapter 8: In the Final Analysis 119

Conclusion 131

DEDICATION

This book is dedicated to my virtuous wife for her love and tireless effort to see that I do well in every endeavor, including this book. She has been my steadfast encourager, my good support, and a wonderful companion. I love you, Dinah.

To my two children, who always reminded me to keep on writing and actually gauged my progress. They kept me motivated because of their interest in seeing this project come to fruition. I could not have given up on this project because of them. Thank you, Andre and Adamma. You will always remain dear to my heart, and I know your God has a lot in store for you. I love you, guys.

To my late mother, Jemima Adanma Anukwuem, who lived a gracious life filled with selfless service to her family and community. Thank you for your unconditional love. I grew up to be who I am today because of your nurturing spirit, wise words, and guidance. Even though you are gone, you are the best mom in the world. I love you, Mama.

To my late father, George Iheanetu Anukwuem, for emphasizing the importance of education. Thank you for your foresight. I love you, Papa.

PREFACE

I came to America in 1998, and by 2006, I was approximately $500,000 in debt. How could any reasonable person accumulate that much debt in such a short time? Very easily. If you buy two new cars and a huge house in a space of two years, and then follow that with consistently reckless spending using borrowed money in an effort to live the American dream, you will end up buried in debt as I was.

Many people get trapped in this so-called dream that turns into a nightmare because they are not mindful of their spending habits. James Truslow Adams defined the American dream in 1931 as the belief that "life should be better and richer and fuller for everyone with opportunity for each according to ability or achievement regardless of social class or circumstances of birth."

Aspiring to live well is noble as long as it is not done at the expense of your future financial stability. If you pursue this dream unintelligently, which is usually the case, the chances are good that you will end up in a financial quagmire. Indeed, it takes poor financial decision making to get neck deep in debt.

Many people are not rich because they get tied up repaying their debts all their working lives. They never make headway and debt sucks the life out of them. Their future earnings are spent servicing their debt, and what if their income stream ceases to flow altogether? How would they react?

Can you rest assured knowing that over the years you have judiciously used your money, paid off outstanding debts in a reasonable time, and have a good amount saved up in your emergency and retirement accounts? Or will you cry foul after you lose your job, even though you worked very hard all those years, due to lack of foresight and reckless use of your money, you have little to show for it? It would be very unfortunate to find yourself in the latter predicament; that would mean you had missed out on the bigger picture. These were the questions I pondered when I realized the depth of my financial problems.

My predicament was obviously my own doing. I had not made wise financial decisions. I lived beyond my means and as a result found myself suffocating in so much debt over time. When after many years I finally recognized I had a problem, I realized I had to tackle it before it got worse.

Problems are solved only when you recognize you have them; you won't seek help for your money problems if you cannot admit you have the vice of spending beyond your means. Just as you cannot ignore the check engine light in your car without risking great damage: the longer you ignore your financial problems, the more they will cost you.

The good news is that there is light at the end of the tunnel. I paid off my crippling debt, and so can you. My advice to you: seize your future and do not mortgage it.

Proverbs 22:7 tells us, "The borrower is a slave to the lender." This statement could not be any further from the truth. I was enslaved by my debts. I would stop in my tracks sometimes because I was suddenly reminded how much I had to pay off. It took the fun and joy out of life. It did not feel good. I had a still, small voice that told me I could become debt free, but I ignored it because paying of my humongous debt seemed an incredible feat. Many times, I talked myself out of believing I could become free of debt. I would casually tell my wife we would pay off our debt in a short period of time even though I did not know how that would happen, but I wanted it to.

Driving home for lunch one day, I heard a voice on the car radio say that paying off all personal debt was doable. If I had not been thinking about becoming debt free, I might not have taken that seriously. The idea that there was a way out excited me, but I knew that any plan to pay down debt would require patience, focus, passion, and discipline. I did not think I measured up in those areas, but I was determined to give it a try. I had been tormented long enough. It was not easy, but three and a half years later, I can proudly say we became debt free.

When I started trying to pay off our debt, I never imagined writing a book about it. I had thought about becoming many things but not an author. Sharing this life-changing experience is an honor and a privilege. I paid off a large amount of debt in a relatively short time; this book will tell you how I came to the realization that debt was a major problem in my life. This book will empower and not discourage you. It will help you seize your future, not mortgage it.

I have not seen any one who loves to owe; it is just not cool, but we make matters worse by continuing to generate more debt. What you do not believe or speak of in faith will never manifest. Think and believe that you will pay off your debt and it will happen. You have to find out what is important in your life. Most of the time, we do very well on those important things when we work on them passionately. What is your passion? What do you want to accomplish? Is being debt free important to you?

As you read this book, remember that we all share similar emotions and experiences. As you read, you will have to figure out who you truly are and what your aspirations are. You will come to understand that life happens and that you need to make the best of what it throws at you. You do not want to muddle it.

You will come to realize the importance of being decisive and doing what is right. Your motivation and patience will be tested anytime you pursue what is dear to your heart. No one said good things come easy. If you do not recognize or admit you have an issue with debt, you'll be unlikely to tackle it. A mentally-ill patient who does not have an insight into his or her problem will probably not seek therapy. You will have to learn to be brutally honest with yourself and examine your habits. Remain content, but do not settle for less—stay committed to solving your financial problems.

What do you consider true wealth? I consider it the knowledge that God is ever present in my life, my loving family, and a content heart. I draw my motivation from my wife and kids, who cheer me on as much as I do them. That is what matters. I encourage you to sacrifice now and enjoy your life more fully when you desperately need to at retirement. I hope and pray that this book makes all the difference in your life.

Godspeed!

CHAPTER 1

Know Who You Are

Who are you really? Have you had moments when you found yourself in a privileged position and wondered if you were out of place? You have worked hard to be where you are, but you continue to have these out-of-body experience in those instances. You have flashbacks of where you came from and compare them to where you are right now.

Sometimes, you cannot come to grips with your changing positions. It is exhilarating and at the same time incredible. If you do not know who you are, you can be overwhelmed by the changing circumstances. Now you are seeing yourself in a different light—I mean humbly, not pompously. You have a new realization of what you can accomplish; you know your dreams can happen if you have enough belief, self-confidence, and perseverance. There is nothing you need to prove because you rest assured in the fact that you were fearfully and wonderfully made according to the Bible.

We are all unique; we have different experiences and thoughts that shape who we are. We do not have to live other people's lives, and we do not let anyone talk us out of our dreams. We learn to enjoy other people's blessings because we are comfortable in who we are, knowing that someday it will be our turn. We cannot be confused anymore; we know we have to be the people God has called us to be.

Where I Started

I grew up in Enugu, a city in southeastern Nigeria, where I completed my elementary and university education. In between, I completed my five-year secondary education in the northern part of the country.

Nigeria is located in west Africa. It is bordered by Niger, Benin, Cameroon, and the Atlantic Ocean. The predominant tribes in Nigeria are the Hausas and Fulanis in the north, the Ibos in the southeast, and the Yorubas in the southwest. Nigeria is regarded as the giant of Africa because of its population and economy. It is the most populous country in Africa with very rich oil reserves. Nigeria is a country with tremendous potential, but unfortunately, corruption continues to stifle real economic growth.

My parents wanted nothing short of a good education for my siblings and me. Education was not an option but a must in my family. In all my years of education, I never learned anything about personal finance, which I now feel should be taught starting in high school everywhere.

During my school years in Nigeria, I focused on passing my exams. I didn't have a part-time job when I was in school, and I do not remember my siblings or friends who did either. It was not the culture back then because there were not too many job opportunities there unlike the Western world. We did not have money to throw around; we had to learn to be content with what we had. Whatever I had I guarded jealously because it was hard to know where the next one will be coming from.

Money was used for things that mattered—food, shelter, clothing, and school books whenever they could be afforded—it was not spent on frivolities. The thinking was that if something wasn't a necessity, you didn't need it. I was one of eighteen children; you can imagine my family had no money to waste. My mom worked very hard for everything we had. She took very little vacation until the latter part of her life, and that was only because her children persuaded her to.

Two decades ago in Nigeria, we did not have credit cards, so we were not tempted to use them and run up huge amounts of debt and incur the stress that comes with that.

Everything was on a cash basis, and that included houses. In those days, I'd see buildings that were half-built and abandoned because the owners' money had run out. In contrast, in the Western world, credit cards or bank loans are more accessible for similar projects. The result is a lot of borrowing that creates an inadvertent debt burden. The credit system obviously creates a false sense of security for those who use it. Consequently, there is a tendency to abuse or overuse it. It will trap you!

One thing I know is that poverty abounds in Nigeria, but debt is rarely the problem. You just lack—you do not really owe! Poverty is not God's intention for our lives. I am fortunate to have experienced life in both worlds. I can confidently say that even though these poor folks in Nigeria lack electricity, water, and even three square meals on a consistent basis, they still carry on like they have the best of life. They are still able to find an inner joy that sustains them. I would not trade the life I lead now in the United States with life anywhere else, but I want some of that unconditional joy Nigerians enjoy, on a regular basis.

Debt accumulates quickly in the credit-card world and can sure tamper with your peace of mind and financial progress. I lived in Nigeria for almost three decades and was debt free. How was I able to accumulate about a half million dollars in debt in only eight years of living in the

United States? It happened to me, and it can happen to others if they don't exercise vigilance.

I lost the freedom from debt I enjoyed in Nigeria in pursuit of the American dream. My standard of living here is by far better than what it was in Nigeria, but that was due to borrowed money.

I have paid off my debt, thanks to God. I started paying it off once I faced up to it and the monumental emotional and physical crippling effect it was having on me. When you realize enough is enough, you'll be on your way to beating the odds. The United States as a country has given me countless opportunities and continues to do so. I have seen both worlds, and I like it better here except for the debt trap I fell into. In the coming chapters you will see how easy it is to fall into that trap.

My Dreams

Dreams may seem unrealistic, but they are powerful driving forces in life. I am not talking about the dreams we have at night, but our daydreams that fuel our ambitions, aspirations, and ideals. It is up to us all to nurture this driving force that will either create a winner or a loser.

The Webster dictionary defines a dream as "to think about something that you wish would happen or something that you want to do or be." Dreams are conceived, watered by meditation, and made real by concerted action. I have had many dreams, one of which was to live in the United States, a dream I had when I was a child. I told my mom I would live in America one day just as some of my brothers and sisters were doing at the time.

My achievements in school were due to my small and big dreams. Life would be meaningless without dreams. My dreams represented my hopes. Near the end of secondary school, I wanted to study medicine, but that meant I'd have to study hard to pass my exams, and that would require hard work and perseverance. I achieved my dream of becoming a medical doctor. Our dreams are our aspirations that we hope would materialize. If we are patient enough and keep working and hoping, our dreams will almost always come true.

Soon after completing medical school, I resurrected my dream of going to America. My goal was to practice medicine there and improve my standard of living. God always has the perfect plan. He knows what we need and gives it to us in an orderly manner and at the perfect time. If I had moved to the United States prematurely, I probably would have been less educated and ill prepared to face the challenges that America would have thrown at me.

Do not lose the essence of your dream; write it down. I cannot explain it, but something divine happens that brings forth your dreams when you write them down. I wrote down almost all of mine as I conceived them. For instance, I wrote down my desire to live and practice medicine in the United States in my medical school yearbook.

I heard a preacher say that to get to God takes a thousand steps, but if you take the first one, he will take the 999 others. A lot rings true in that statement. To achieve anything in life, you have to put something in motion first. I took the first part of the foreign medical graduate examination in medical school that would allow me to enter a residency training program in the United States. It was my first step toward my aspiration; I knew God would orchestrate the other steps at his own perfect timing.

There is no promise that your dreams will come true when you want them to. Dreams can take a month, a year, a decade, or even a lifetime to come to fruition. My dreams did not happen on my timetable; it took me an extra year to get into medical school, even though I would have loved for it to have happened sooner but I did not give up on it. It took four years after graduating from medical school to come to the United States. It took a couple of years after passing my foreign medical graduate exams before getting into a residency training program. I can go on and on. You can quit on your dreams or fight for them—it's that simple. Waiting for your dream may seem unpleasant at the time, but it will be very gratifying when it comes to fruition.

You do not have to live out other people's dream; if you try to, you will lose the true meaning of personal ambition. When I flew into Newark International airport from Lagos, Nigeria, I checked off another of my dreams accomplished. I saw my brothers and sisters living out their dreams. That motivated me to do well, but I soon realized America was not a bed of roses. I had to work very hard for every cent I earned. In contrast, I had seen Nigerians get a full day's pay without putting a commensurate amount of time at work.

My new life was ahead of me; I wanted to live well. I had seen other people do it, and I was determined to as well. It was only a few years later that I had gotten married to a beautiful woman, had two lovely children, and bought two new cars and a nice house.

There is nothing wrong with seeking a good life; I did so diligently and honestly. But in year eight, I was about $500,000 in the hole. Be careful what you desire because even if it's good, if you go about it the wrong way, you could get yourself in trouble. I had overused my credit and did not have a clear plan to pay off my debt. I quickly realized that money did not grow on trees in America. It was obvious that I had pursued my dream honestly but used the wrong approach to do that.

Make sure your dreams are reasonable. Pursue them with caution as well as diligence. Establish a concrete plan to attain your dream without getting up to your neck in debt. Your dreams will fashion your life, so never cease dreaming. I dreamed that one day I would pay off our debt, and I did because I had dreamed of becoming debt free.

America Offers a Good Life

My medical school training was grueling. I had to pass exams to progress to the next level, so I studied with focus and urgency. I did not want to be left behind; I wanted to become a medical doctor.

One of my many exams was regarded as the mother of all examinations. Passing this particular one meant that most assuredly I'd fulfill my dream of becoming a doctor. A few of my classmates who flunked this examination were kicked out of medical school. It is easily considered the toughest examination in medical school. It was an intense time. The exam was the first of four major exams. Those who passed it had what it took to remain a medical student. Preparing for this exam required brains, focus, and intensity.

Most students gave it all they had and revved up their preparation a few weeks to months before the exam. I was not an exception. Two weeks before this important exam, we had a citywide power outage that lasted for those two weeks. I studied by lantern and candlelight. It turned out all right for me at the end of the day.

In Nigeria power outages are the norm and not the exception. You can go days at a time without power many times in a month. With all the oil money, the brilliance and intelligence of the Nigerian people, you expect that it would and should be better. Unfortunately, the country has continued to struggle in the areas of power and water supply as well as the road system.

In contrast, I have been in the United States now for approximately two decades. I have been through perhaps ten power outages, and they rarely lasted a long time. There has been a constant water supply in my eighteen years in America. Perhaps the culture of maintenance is alive and well here. In America, food is abundant that it is not surprising America ranks number one in the list of top ten most obese countries. Most of the poor here are richer than most people of the world when it comes to material possession. Most households could boast of a car, a television, and a steady water and power supply. It is easy to take these basic needs for granted in the States, whereas lack of them is the norm in so many other parts of the world.

It's not surprising that people give up the worlds they know to immigrate to the United States. I watched a movie recently; the main character was a Nigerian forensic pathologist played by a renowned American actor. The character said many rank heaven number one and the United States a close second. I can relate to that.

In the United States, anything is possible—the sky's the limit here. But the sky sometimes comes with a price. You're expected to work hard, and some do so diligently with much discipline and conscientiousness. They are also disciplined enough to use their money to afford this goodness wisely. Unfortunately, they constitute a subset; the majority of people get carried away by the American way of life and pursue it with a less-than-clever approach. They live it with loans and credit cards. My friend and classmate during our residency years in New York realized the traps that credit cards presented, so he stopped using them. I wish I had had his discipline back then, but I do now.

Keeping Up with the Joneses

Humans are naturally copycats. Part of our nature is to fight to belong, compete, prove a point, and do as well if not better than the next person. It is no wonder that most people will do whatever it takes to live the good life—sometimes against their better judgment or even at the expense of their future livelihood.

It is common to see neighbors, friends, or even siblings flaunt their material possessions to prove they have arrived. Quite often the copycats do not know the financial wherewithal of those they emulate and consequently spend much more than they can afford. This behavior is more rampant than we know. Keeping up with the Joneses is an American pastime; it is an infectious societal disease. We consciously and subconsciously participate in this behavior every day.

Several years ago, I moved to North Carolina with my wife and kids to begin a primary care practice. Another physician worked nearby. She had just graduated from a residency program and drove an older car. Before I moved down, I had worked two years in post-residency training. I may have earned more than she had in the previous two years. I drove a new luxury car at that time. A few months after her first encounter with my new car, she ditched her older car for something newer. It could have been coincidental, but prior to buying the newer car, she had complimented me a few times on my car. I believe that her encounter with my newer car influenced her behavior.

People always want to be perceived as doing well, and that can cause others to want to be perceived the same way. Most times, they justify buying something newer or better by telling themselves that if so-and-so can do so, so can they. And that desire might cause us to lose sight of the financial implications of our actions.

We play this game sometimes to fit in or gain attention. We must understand who we are and what we can and can't afford. We often misrepresent ourselves a lot. Materialism is the least of what makes us who we are; nevertheless, we desperately chase this facade because we learn quickly that society judges us based on our perceived status. It is a learned behavior that can easily take over our lives.

A few months after I completed my residency program, I bought my wife and kids a new minivan. Not too long after, I bought that luxury sedan. I had just become a full-fledged physician and felt I had to play the part. I thought our family of four needed a minivan, but that could have been influenced by what I had heard other families of a similar size said about a minivan. A smaller car would have handled our transportation needs. In hindsight, buying those vehicles was a matter of poor judgment; I was paying a lot every month to keep up with the Joneses.

When we get the desire to copy or keep up with others, we do not worry that they might be in a better financial position; all we worry about is appearing the same. That thought germinates and grows; it is fed by commercials and window shopping as well, and then we act on it—we buy what we do not need or more than we need.

We have friends who have kids about the same ages as ours. When it comes to dance lessons, karate, basketball, piano and singing lessons, movies—you name it—you can be sure we are along for the ride. Our better judgment told us all these activities were nibbling away at our money, but we would convince ourselves that we did not want our children to feel left behind.

Other parents get caught up in this dilemma. If they are not mindful, they get suckered into this behavior time and again. We have been there too many times. And the temptation to be copycats is much stronger in affluent neighborhoods populated by high-income earners and spenders. But if you dig deeper, you'll discover that many of these people have abysmal net worth. I can tell you that because we were one of them!

The behavior of being a copycat creeps up on us because we allow it to. It costs us precious time and money. Until you can come to terms with who you are and how much money you actually have, the chances are good that you will continue to feel like you're defined by your material possessions or the activities you engage your kids in. Trust me, it is very easy to be suckered into this wasteful lifestyle.

Just recently, a couple we know had a new baby. They already had a couple of kids; their last child was over ten years old. Since then, our ten-year-old daughter has been pestering my wife and me to have a third baby. She obviously does not completely comprehend all that goes into having a baby. We reminded her that just because a neighbor buys a new car doesn't mean we have to. If we had no complaints with our current vehicles, it would make no sense to replace it. Our reasoning with our daughter showed a level of maturity on our part; we had developed a different mental attitude toward that kind of pressure. It was an analogy my daughter completely understood. My wife and I are now free from this pestering. Thank God!

Copy what works for you, not what works for anyone else. Keeping up with the Joneses is alive and well. Physicians epitomize this behavior very well. I am one and have been around other doctors long enough to speak confidently. If they are not flaunting a new, expensive gadget or acquisition, they are bragging about the vacation they just took or about to take. Such behavior leads to a low net worth and a bleak financial future, and that cuts across all classes of people.

Stand by what you believe, know who you are, and do not live any other person's life.

CHAPTER 2

Do Not Fool Yourself

Being overconfident is as bad as the opposite. We act recklessly when we think we know it all. We can live in fool's paradise all we want, but life is about being realistic. We set and achieve goals and dreams by conscientious effort; we have to work hard, not fool ourselves or expect freebies.

Life has consequences; we reap what we sow. We must avoid unrealistic expectations. I cannot do wrong all year and expect good to come out of it; I guarantee it just does not work like that. Good attitudes, behaviors, and habits almost always yield favorable results. We must keep our expectations reasonable and not fool around.

Life Happens

We all face life's ups and downs; they do not discriminate. We live in an imperfect world. Whether you are white, brown, or black, life happens. Your creed will not exonerate you either; Matthew 5:45 tells us, "For He gives his sunlight to both the evil and the good and He sends rain on the just and the unjust alike."

Life is generally good for the most part, but we all have and will face setbacks here and there. Our reaction or inaction to adversity will determine whether we win or lose in this life. I play golf, and I've played good and bad rounds in my many years as an amateur golfer. I accepted the days I played poorly with a heavy heart. Yes! Golf can stir up emotions, but I have never thrown my clubs in a fit. What has kept me going back and golfing again after a bad round is my determination to improve my game. Golfers will tell you that one great shot after any number of bad shots is what keeps them coming back to the game. Understand that without setbacks in life, we might never develop to our full potential. We have to accept life's challenges and move on. I have learned to dwell on those moments of goodness that remind me life is worth living.

I lived in New York for three years and had my fair share of setbacks. I hit a pothole one day while driving home from work. It was a dark night, and it was drizzling. I had left the hospital as usual after a tedious day. Every time I left work, I always wanted to get home in time to relax and hit the sack.

I heard a rattling under my car. Turns out I had broken the axle. That cost me $500, and I wasn't earning much then. You have probably faced an air conditioner breaking down or the microwave not working or a relative who's taken sick. Have you noticed these problems come in waves that can be overwhelming? They can cost you hundreds if not thousands of dollars. Unfortunately, that is life. They can deal an average family a major financial blow they cannot do anything about immediately.

Ironically, at times like those, you appreciate having a good line of credit so you can handle the immediate problem, but then you are straddled with debt that could take you years to pay back considering the interest rates.

But when you do not have good credit that will give you some wiggle room, that can be scary. If you spend indiscriminately on frivolities, you will not have a fighting chance against unexpected and expensive problems that can make it even harder to save up for emergencies. I am writing from experience because I have been there. I blamed myself for so many of those instances because I left myself vulnerable due to my poor financial choices. I thought that maybe if I did not have any credit card debt, I probably would be in a better position to absorb some of these shocks. I also thought that if I spent below my means, maybe I would not be overly anxious during these difficult times. I had no shock absorber mechanism, plain and simple. I knew things had to change and quick.

Life will continue to push us to the limit. Now that we know these things, what are we going to do about it? Will we change our spending habits to gain some wiggle room for when the unexpected comes knocking? Will we discipline ourselves financially? Will we examine our motivation for our expenses and not live paycheck to paycheck?

We all should establish solid financial goals and identify the roadblocks that keep us from financial independence. Life is not so far spent that we cannot make honest mental changes. We have not been promised an easy life; it is up to us to turn things around to our benefit. Debt stole my peace of mind; I have chosen to live differently; I fought to pay off my debt.

Every day is a struggle not to get back in debt. Debt beclouds our outlook on life and makes it difficult to fend off the darts life throws our way. In the coming chapters, I will be looking at attitude changes that helped me become debt free.

Do What Is Right

When one good decision follows another, goals are achieved. There has to be the decision first, and many right things have to be in alignment to create the building blocks needed for success.

Anything we do in life can be categorized as right or wrong. Consistency in doing right almost always fosters a good life. Wrongdoing might look okay for the time being, but in due course, because you are building on a shaky foundation, what you are trying to accomplish will fail. Our actions have consequences.

Every day, I struggle to do what is right. I know what is right, but for some reason, I have sometimes gravitated to things that are not. I got into a mountain of debt because of a series of wrong choices. I made poor choices in matters of our personal finances because I was more concerned with instant gratification. Doing right always appeared harder because it required more discipline and sacrifice. We are influenced by our environment and our society more than ever; there is more tolerance for the wrong things nowadays. More and more people are doing whatever makes them happy regardless if it is wrong. Our society preaches this new paradigm, and it can very easily rub off on an unprincipled mind.

I have counseled several of my patients about their smoking. Nine out of ten receive my advice well, but others say, "Doctor, I don't drink, I don't chase after women, I don't party, so why must I give up the one thing I enjoy?" And then these people end up in the hospital due to an acute flare-up of a chronic lung disease caused by smoking. They put up this baseless argument despite a good knowledge of their medical condition.

In the same vein, I have justified a huge house, a nice car, even though it had put me heftily in debt. You cannot continue to get away when you dabble in the wrong stuff. You cannot continue to fool yourself; years of poor choices eventually show up in your life and finances. Just as chronic smokers can end up carrying around oxygen tanks, high spenders carry around huge debt and the huge psychological burden that comes with it. Financial emergencies keep them from taking advantage of favorable business opportunities and being able to give charitably; in extreme cases, smokers will die and those in debt will have to declare bankruptcy.

It all starts with the first puff of a cigarette or the first unnecessary expenditure, and it grows from there. Little drops of water make a mighty ocean, as the saying goes. I have always kicked myself after making impulsive purchases but still on occasion find myself making them.

In our society, oftentimes we call right wrong and wrong right. We always find good excuses when we do that. We have to do what is just, good, and proper with our money. Selfishness, keeping up with the Joneses, stubbornness, discontent, and ingratitude are all wrong for our financial health. These poor choices were detrimental to my progress.

There is nothing right about living beyond our means. It is not right to spend tomorrow's money today. It is not right to spend what we should save. It is not right to be self-consumed. I got into debt willfully and purposefully by doing wrong. I had to consciously shut out the voice that constantly justified all my wrongdoing.

I have always encouraged my kids to tell the truth. I tell them that if they make good choices, truth comes easy and naturally. I have caught them at times struggling to tell the truth. When I asked them why, they would say they did not want to get in trouble for doing wrong. Ironically, they tell a fib thinking it will get them out of trouble. It is always easy to tell when they are being less than honest; I stress the fact that they will always be fine with the truth rather than half-truths or lies.

We are not perfect people; we will have to fight to do right, but we can gain an inner peace and satisfaction by doing right. My kids understand that doing right produces good consequences and wrongdoing bad consequences. Doing right reinforces the behavior. If nothing else, do right for the sake of it.

If wrong gets you in trouble, why not choose right and skip off unscathed? Paul tells us in Romans 7:19, "For I do not do the good I want to do, but the evil I do not want to do, this I keep on doing." I pray we strive to do what is right in every area of our lives and not just our finances. I pray we pursue what is good and right.

Examine Your Habits

What are your habits? When was the last time you paid attention to them? Do some of your habits get in the way of your financial health? What habits are you struggling with? Bad habits negatively impact your life. To take charge, you must examine your habits.

We subconsciously repeat certain behavior patterns that shape our lives for good or bad. When we begin to look carefully at our everyday life, we will see it is filled with many habits. Some of our habits help us get through the day, and we share the same habits with many others. If you are like me, you hit the snooze button a few times before you get up. We also have habits that are unique to us.

If you are honest, you would admit to good and bad habits and admit that you have to practice your good habits so you retain them, and that your bad habits are holding you back. If you are unsure of what your habits are, ask someone who is close to you; others can be more aware of your habits than you are. Do not dismiss others' observations as you might typically do; their observations might be your only eyes to the truth.

Smoking, gluttony, excessive alcohol consumption, lying, and procrastination are all bad habits, and there are many more, of course. Usually, nothing good comes out of a bad habit, but we can acknowledge it, reject it, and empower others to do the same. That is, if we survive the habit in the first place.

Smokers pay a heavy price for their bad habit in terms of the dollars they spend to indulge in the habit for years and years, and then in terms of what they pay to try to manage the cancer, heart attacks, circulatory problems, strokes, pregnancy problems, and chronic lung diseases that can result from smoking. I have often told my patients that this habit will not add a single day to their lifespan.

Some habits can condemn us to a life of mediocrity. Take for example procrastination, which I will discuss in later chapters. I can relate well to this behavior because I thrived on holding off important projects until the eleventh hour for frivolous reasons. I felt unsettled and rushed all the time, and that created unnecessary anxiety. Some might not think this is a problem, but it is more rampant than we think. Procrastination when it comes to studying can produce average students who will be forever affected financially by that.

Gluttony causes obesity, which comes with health and financial consequences. I have heard that airlines charge morbidly obese passengers double or triple the airfare to accommodate their size. The amount of money spent treating obese patients is phenomenal. There is no winning with gluttony. Proverbs 23:20–22 tells us, "Do not join those who drink too much wine or gorge themselves on meat, for drunkards and gluttons become poor, and drowsiness clothes them in rags."

Lying might come easily, but it can alienate us from genuine friends. I do not want to be labeled a liar. I have seen people get mugged and killed on the streets in Third World countries for stealing or lying. Excessive drinking is also a habit with huge financial and health implications. Just name a bad habit and you can find a major consequence of it.

On the other hand, good habits result in good outcomes. By all accounts, getting up early is a good habit, though I have struggled with that. But when I get a jump on the day, I can get so much more accomplished. Overachievers are probably early birds.

Working hard and reading are good habits that pay dividends. Hard work is as important as talent. Humans are not equals; our talents are different, but whatever we lack in talent, we can make up for by hard work.

Whether they are good or bad, habits are easy to form. Repeat a behavior two or three times and you will make it a habit. This, however, includes giving into an urge to make an impulse purchase; that could ultimately lead to impoverishment.

The good news is that habits can be broken. You do that by relearning that bad habit. My wife and I indulged in impulse buying, which created the mess we found ourselves in for a while. As part of the "cleaning up our habits" mentality, we cornered this particular habit and nipped it in the bud. We consciously stopped buying things arbitrarily. Anything we bought was planned, and we even tried very hard not to deviate from our grocery lists. Just as you formed the habit in the first place, resist it once, twice, thrice, and you are on your way to replacing the bad habit with a good one. We cannot fool ourselves; habits shape our lives, and bad habits must be recognized and dealt with forthrightly.

Most of our bad habits temporarily fulfill a desire or fill a void. For the period you are engaged in it, you feel good, but consider how it will affect your life over the long run. Discover what is not going well in your life; it could be due to a bad habit that needs eradication. And remember to reinforce your good habits. You cannot continue to live in a fool's paradise. If you see hindrances to your ability to achieve debt freedom, look for the habits that might be contributing to that; until you acknowledge them, you won't be able to change them.

Living on the Edge

A few months ago, I was sitting in the physician's lounge during a well-deserved break with a colleague. We got to talking about how expensive things had become. We agreed that people's earnings were not keeping up with inflation and how people were struggling financially.

A recent survey by bankrate.com reported that as many as three-quarters of Americans live paycheck to paycheck with little to no emergency money tucked away. I was definitely part of this statistic. When I was in my medical residency training, I was not earning much, but it should have been enough. It was in part because I lived beyond my means. New York is expensive, granted, but in hindsight, I could have ditched my car and made other financial adjustments so my monthly pay would cover my monthly expenses.

But I piled up credit card debt. I had my fair share of unexpected expenses that kept me worried; my heart pounded, and I worried about how to solve this and that problem and when the next one would come. That happened month after month. It reached the point that I struggled to make the minimum payment. I did not want to default.

I dreaded receiving every bill. I did not have any reprieve to this problem of living paycheck to paycheck and right on the edge. It was a problem I had created, and it was draining my energy.

It is easy to think that those with high incomes are exempt from such problems, but that is untrue. I started earning more after finishing my residency, but by then, I was in debt up to my knees. Regardless, like most people who get a raise, I revved up my spending, and the vicious cycle continued. I again ended up living from hand to mouth. And that can happen to anyone regardless of race, gender, creed, or salary.

We are blinded to reality when we make more money because for some reason we feel invincible. There is a satisfaction and thrill that come with acquiring material things, but I always worry about how I will pay them off. These mixed emotions feel like the times I have waited anxiously to get on a roller coaster. I do not care how many times I ride on one, I feel the same butterflies in my belly, pounding heart, and dry mouth. During the ride itself, there is an overwhelming thrill and excitement that accounts for why people will stand in long lines for a ride on one.

People definitely enjoy this lifestyle even though it can be very detrimental to their financial viability. If you keep on doing the same thing, you should not expect a different outcome. I wanted to live in the moment; I wanted what I wanted. I did not want to feel deprived. I saw the financial difficulty that it was causing me, but I chose to live in a fool's paradise.

At some point, I had to ask myself some tough questions. Is this my best life? Debt was kind of killing me, and I had made it worse by using borrowed money without real plans on how to pay it off. I had to do something better to change this vicious cycle of living on the edge. I had to recognize what was going on and address it. It took self-encouragement and desire, but the change did not come easy—not at all.

Credit Card Trap

The credit card is ingeniously thought out. It is a goldmine for the creditors. They count on your overusing your card and carrying a balance they can charge you interest on every month. Credit cards can offer limits that are too high for the salaries that are supposed to pay them off. This is a trap people fall into day in and day out—financing the American dream with credit cards.

What exactly is a credit card? A credit card is a type of payment card used predominantly in the Western world. The user is called the card holder. With the credit card you can purchase goods and services on the holder's promise to pay them back. The bank is the financial institution that issues these cards, granting the card holder a line of credit and in this way the holder can borrow money for payment to merchants and stores that accept this form of payment. The credit card can also be used for cash advances. You may also hear of a score assigned to the holder in order to stratify their credit worthiness. A higher score means that you are looked at favorably and considered a low-risk borrower.

I rejoiced when a department store issued me my first credit card years ago. You may have thought I struck gold if you had seen me then. I did not have to justify purchasing my needs, and I talked myself into buying my wants. At some point, the difference between the two became fuzzy. That was my undoing.

I used it more and more because of its convenience. I guessed making the minimum payment on my card was all it took to remain in good standing with the creditor. I quickly forgot myself. I developed a false sense of security with my card. I had cultivated a dependence mentality on the credit card. It was not apparent at the beginning, but down the line, it became clear I was addicted to it. Very few people recognize this behavior and are judicious with their cards. They understand how to take advantage of some of the benefits of the credit card, and they pay off their balances monthly to avoid additional charges. I was far from being such a consumer.

I was always very mindful not to overshoot my line of credit. I succeeded in that but failed to keep my debt down. I carried an average balance of at least 50 percent of my credit line. When creditors see that you are keeping up with payments, they boost your line of credit. Mine went from $500 initially to $1,000 and on up. My spending also increased commensurately. I became a master of rationalizing all my silly purchases; I would tell myself, *I can afford the monthly minimum* and *You live only once.*

It did not take me long to take on a substantial debt. It never crossed my mind to pay off my balance monthly, so I incurred interest charges on my unpaid balance. It became a vicious cycle. I lived as if I made more money than I actually did. I could not save or invest. I thought about my debt every day. Most of my income was earmarked to service my debt. The American dream had turned into a nightmare. I could not shake it off. I compounded my problems by lying to myself. I was trapped. Can you relate?

CHAPTER 3

Change Your Mentality

So many articles and books deal with how powerful the mind is. We know firsthand that what we have between our ears can keep us happy or sad and can make us overachievers or underachievers. If you want to change your life, you must change how you think, as we have heard quite often. If we have conflicting thoughts, we are bound to make mistakes often.

We make things that matter to us a priority because of our mind-sets. Rain or shine, we tune out distractions to accomplish what we consider the most important. If we have a misguided thought about our big paycheck buying us wealth, surely it will happen, but at whose expense? Think like a mediocre person and your life will be filled with mediocrity. We are most powerful when we use our mind positively. Every great thing that has ever been invented or created has come from a conceived thought. We change our mentality by feeding our mind what we truly want our lives to be like. We need to think always but positively.

A Big Paycheck Does Not Guarantee Great Wealth

I have always had a twisted interpretation of what wealth meant to me. I thought wealth meant just material possessions. Knowing what I know now, I can brag on my wealth only based on the difference between what I earn and what I spend. You are as wealthy as whatever you can keep of your salary. Show me your net worth, and I will tell you how rich you are.

I was among those who thought a big salary meant great wealth. People commonly equate more money to more buying power. That is true, but like most addictive behavior, the chances are that with a bigger paycheck, you will spend more and more and more. It is a deceptive mentality that very easily can get us in real financial messes. This behavior got me in one, and that is why I wrote this book. Big man, big trouble was a popular saying where I grew up. It means that the more you earn, the bigger your problems will be or the more problems you will attract to yourself. Most addictive people do not purposely go out to become addicted; they will say their behavior was initially benign, just for the fun of it. Unfortunately, they get hooked through repetition of the behavior and eventually cannot function without it. The same action brings less and less fulfillment, so they engage in it all that much more to get the original effect. This eventually becomes a full-fledged addictive behavior. Addiction is not just limited to recreational drugs, prescription drugs, coffee, pornography, or video games; spendthrifts are bona fide members of this group.

That is why it does not matter how much you earn but rather how much you keep. The average American household earns about $34,000 a year. I have earned below and above that amount. What surprised me was that no matter how much I was earning, I always overspent my income and felt I never had enough. I wanted more each time I got a raise. Part of me enjoyed the buying power that more money afforded me, but another part of me knew it was an abuse of power. I may have acquired more material possessions, but I did not feel rich. This desire to buy any and everything cuts across all levels of income, and it can lead anyone to poverty. If I had not checked this mentality, I probably would not have ever been in the position to write about this.

It is human to desire more; no wonder we hear about the supposedly superrich in Hollywood filing bankruptcy because of an insatiable appetite for more. Big man, big trouble! I heard of a superstar who had a fifty-room home and a fleet of cars but ultimately had to declare bankruptcy. This inability to remain content is not peculiar to the superrich; most of us possess this negative trait. We do many stupid things when we think we have money and recklessly spend because we feel we can.

Change your mentality. Live below your means. Take advantage of your income, no matter what it is, and pay down your debt. You can become what you truly desire in your heart.

I wanted to become financially free. At the rate I was going, that would have been impossible. I started looking at money differently. I began to use it wisely. I now know what it takes. I am rich based on what I keep, not on how much I make or spend. Remember that!

Do Not Be Mediocre—Be Fanatical

Mediocrity is a result of poor time management, nonchalance, lack of foresight, unbelief, self-doubt, and fearfulness. Mediocre people are underachievers; they consciously and subconsciously sabotage their own progress. The average Joe feels no pressure to perform; he knows attention is not directed at him, so he basks in this seemingly safe place. He hates this but continues to fuel this negative behavior for some reason. All he needs to do is recognize this regressive behavior and change his outlook on life, but he cannot help the halfhearted commitment. I have been there and have had to fight this negative attitude.

Many times, I could have done better but chose to be mediocre. I have had trouble managing my time effectively. It was quite evident in my school days; back then, I allowed distractions and used many excuses to keep from completing tasks on time. I was not a bad student, but my approach needed smoothing. I got into the habit of waiting until the last minute to tackle projects or study for an exam. Ironically, I wanted to do well, but I thought and acted like a mediocre person who was content to cram at the last minute. There is no benefit to that style; you are always stuck with an uphill task. In contrast, I felt so much better, confident, and at peace whenever I was proactive because I was not pressured by time. It was night and day with the latter approach.

A few years ago, I was due to take my American Board of Internal Medicine (ABIM) recertification examination by December 2014. For the most part, exams are anxiety provoking for me, and that feeling is compounded if I have not prepared in a timely fashion. I worked full-time then and had to squeeze out all the time that I could for study. I took advantage of the provision by ABIM that gave the examinee an opportunity to take the exam two or three years earlier. Though I had a busy schedule, I had ample, stress-free time to study, and I passed. I could not have done it any better.

Most people desire to do well, but if their effort is halfhearted, they might as well forget about it! It does not matter how intelligent you think you are, you have to pay your dues. I did not see paying off our debt as urgent at the time, so I just sat on it.

I have two adorable kids who try to do their best most of the time. Like most kids in America, they are very privileged and blessed. We keep them always engaged in one activity or the other. My wife and I did not have as many opportunities as do kids nowadays. I have closely observed my children's engagements and interests and saw they excelled in areas that interested them and performed average in the areas they did not particularly care about. Once they are interested, you can count on their giving it their all; if they are uninterested, it is like pulling teeth to get them engaged.

When they were three and four, we enrolled them in a dojo. Because of their intense interest, they excelled and went on to earn black belts. They gave 110 percent at every class and competition. They exemplified what a sensei wanted in a student. They were leaders in their class, and their peers looked up to them. It was a true joy whenever we watched them perform. We had different parents come to us to ask what made them so good. Our response was simple—they loved it, and so they practiced every day with a passion. We even had to ask them occasionally to relax from always practicing. They squeezed in a practice any chance they could get. When you are interested in something, the sky is the limit, but if you are content with just going through the motions, you will be mediocre. I had no interest in paying off my debts, so I did not.

I now have the bigger picture of my life. Without foresight, you run in circles. I am motivated by my dreams and aspirations. I had to have a plan for all the major accomplishments in my life; nothing was ever thrown into my lap. You see results when you are dedicated and have a plan and a direction, not when you make random guesses. That is not how God meant it to be. I did not have foresight about our debt, so I dealt with it haphazardly, and the result was more debt. I realized I had to visualize where I wanted to go. Motivational speakers and financiers will ask you where you see yourself in a month, a year, and ten years from now. It is always hard to wrap our hands around huge goals or goals far off in the future. Do not allow the big picture to overwhelm you to the point of mediocrity. Take your goals one step at a time, and do not get ahead of yourself; that will increase the chances you will reach them.

Fear can paralyze you; it will always be an enemy to your progress. Fear and doubt go hand in hand. Hebrews 11:1 tells us that faith is the "substance of things hoped for, the evidence of things not seen." On the contrary, fear is the substance of things not hoped for and the evidence of things and experiences seen in the past. Fear is perverted faith.

Fear stems from negative life experiences and a lack of trust in God's promises. I am fearful when I focus on the wrong things, when I doubt my abilities, when I am more concerned about how other people perceive me. I constantly have to fight fear because it can keep me from realizing my true potential and becoming all my God has called me to be.

I brooded over my debt and worried about achieving debt freedom as quickly as I wanted to. If I had allowed that fear to take root, it would have paralyzed me. But I did not let my fear take root; I chipped away at my debt month by month, year by year until it was paid off in about three and half years, less time than I had projected.

Do not listen to naysayers; they could plant seeds of doubt and prevent you from achieving your dream. Learn to spot them and run away from them.

Fanaticism can have a negative connotation; as far as I remember, this word has always been used in the context of religion and its followers. It has been abused; in my mind, the word *bigot* would better describe those people. *Webster's* defines fanaticism as excessive enthusiasm with intense, uncritical devotion. I consider fanaticism a good thing.

My fanaticism about getting rid of my debt made that possible. I needed enthusiasm and passion to confront and conquer my negative financial environment. I did not entertain a single negative thought about it. I saw vividly where I was heading. I realized the implications of remaining in debt and understood the benefits of being financially independent. I had debt freedom in my sights. And my fanaticism about this rubbed off on my wife.

Life holds too much in store for us. We cannot achieve our full potential being mediocre. Every day I remind myself to focus on what is right. I tell myself to remain motivated and enthused every step of the way. Nobody will push our agendas but us. Granted, life will send us our share of ups and downs, but it will be up to us to keep fighting and never give up.

My Motivation

Any major accomplishment in life requires motivation. All our actions are due to our motivations. Unmotivated people are unsuccessful people. If you want to wallow in mediocrity, stay unmotivated. Self-doubt kills motivation, while motivation propels you to action. My motivation prompted me to write this book to share with others. Likewise, I was able to become debt free because I was pushed by several motivations.

First, I had to be brutally honest with myself. I could not ignore my predicament. We owed big and had to do something about it. I looked at the consequences of having to pay down my debt all my life and did not like it. I knew that clinging to our debt for a long time came with major financial implications. I started using money I could have invested to pay down my debt plus interest charges. The longer I took to pay off our debts, the slower I could start investing; I did not want to cling to our debt for any longer than I had to. I wanted to do it in three or four years rather than thirty or forty years. I could not start saving up a decent nest egg until my debts were paid in full. I was motivated to pay as little interest on my debt as I could; I wanted to keep as much of my money as I could.

After so many years of work, I would want to have something to show for it. The difference between doing well during retirement and not doing well is how much you were able to save, and I wanted to save as much as I could. I knew the sooner I was out of debt, the sooner I could start saving and investing for retirement. I do not want to be broke when I need money most.

I wanted to be a good steward of the money God sent my way. Remember the parable of the talents? A master gave his servants talents according to their abilities. One received ten talents, one received five, and the last received one. The one with ten and the one with five doubled those amounts, but the servant with one talent had buried it. When the master returned, he rewarded the first two but took away the one talent from the third. We too need to be wise enough to make the best of our gifts. If we are lazy, the consequences of laziness will befall us. Like a good and faithful servant, I want to account for all the money when it is required of me, and I know you wish the same.

Second, I was working under duress because my bills were strangling me. That can take the fun out of work. I wanted to be a doctor because I loved what I did; I wasn't there just to collect a paycheck. On top of that, my stress deprived me of truly enjoying my family. I wanted more time with my family; that is precious time. The burden of debt and the fact that I was working hard because I had to robbed me of this precious family time.

I have worked very hard these past few years to get out of debt in a reasonable time frame; I didn't want to work myself to death; I didn't want my work to put me in a negative mind frame and make me unfriendly. My lovely wife and two kids need me as much as I need them. Nowadays, I am much more effective and sharper at work; being debt free, I can focus on what truly matters—being the best doctor, husband, and father I can be and being happy. Money cannot buy that.

Third, I wanted to travel. And I still do, even with the current negative state of world affairs. I feel I will realize this dream. Traveling will definitely broaden my knowledge and increase my appreciation of other peoples and their cultures. I believe the world will heal better if people travel more. However, the constraints of debt can limit our ability to do so.

I have taken a lot for granted since coming to America, but I still have in the back of my mind the disorder that exists where I came from, and that has given me a vast appreciation for life. Maybe we will become less judgmental when we can understand other people who do not speak or look like us. I want to be accommodating just as I have been accommodated here in America. It is my dream to travel far and wide, and that desire has motivated me to tackling my debts with the urgency that it merited.

Fourth, I want to be more charitable. It is human nature to want to keep what you have especially if you are not sure where the next dollar or meal or whatever will come from. It goes against logic to be charitable in dire circumstances. It is sad because those who do not have are desperately clinging on and looking for someone to bless them rather than someone to bless. I grew up in Nigeria where resources and personal wealth are scarce. I guarded what I had and was not looking to bless anyone. But I know now that you do not have to be rich to be a blessing to your neighbor. Galatians 2:10 tells us, "Remember the poor." I want to be a blessing to the less privileged and my church. Giving epitomizes selflessness. Giving is a virtue that opens most doors. There is an inner satisfaction and sense of accomplishment that comes with giving.

I believe part of our purpose on earth is to help others. I want to be more like God, who constantly gives. The problem is that debt can destroy our ability to give. With too much debt, we might give begrudgingly if at all. I desperately desired to free myself from the claws of debt because I noticed that it adversely affected my desire to be charitable.

Last, I wanted peace of mind. There is so much that can affect our peace, and I want money to be way down that list. My debt took away my peace of mind; I easily got overwhelmed, particularly with expensive emergencies that would come up, and it made my already delicate state worse.

Motivations may vary, but they all propel us to take action. What are your motivations? Make them real by writing them out and tape them to your mirror, program them into your smart phone, or even just tuck them in your wallet.

I encourage my overweight patients to constantly keep in mind their reasons for wanting to lose weight. Most of my patients who lost weight did so due to their motivations. If you are motivated, even difficult projects become doable.

Set Goals and Dreams

Life is good, but it comes with a price. God created life so that we could enjoy it but not without doing our part. I do not think that folding our hands and wishing for the best is God's intention for us. He has given us creative minds we can use to achieve a better world. Technology is one example of this. And we would not have been flying if it were not for the creative Wright brothers. Neil Armstrong's walk on the moon was an achievement because someone dared to dream. We are innately wired to seek at least comfortable if not better lives, and we do so by dreaming and improving ourselves.

I long to do well in life and know it will take commitment, patience, sacrifice, and a strong will to achieve that. I have to back up my aspirations and goals by focus and action to realize them. Nothing is thrown into our laps. Proverbs 24:33–34 warns us, "A little sleep, a little slumber, a little folding of the hands to rest and poverty will come on you like a thief and scarcity like an armed man."

Laziness springs from a lack of an understanding of the importance of our purpose, goals, aspirations, and dreams. When we are decisive about our objectives and goals, our direction becomes clear. In the Bible, Joseph's brothers called him a dreamer. He saw his purpose through his dreams and eventually got into Pharaoh's palace through integrity and discipline. I wonder what life would look like without dreams and goals. My belief is that life has so much in store for me. The motivation to live lies in our goals and dreams. Life is about goal setting.

I have been discouraged by the sheer size of some of my dreams. They appear too big and unattainable. How on earth could I pay off close to $500,000 in such a short time? That dream seemed way too grandiose.

But just as I had my overweight patients set short-term, manageable goals, I set small, attainable goals when I started paying off our debt rather than looking at all the money I had to pay off. If you focus on just the next step, not all the steps you have to take, you will achieve the big goal.

Goals are very important. Find someone who will hold you accountable. Go for your goals and dreams without looking back—no regrets. I do not want to be like the forty-, fifty-, and even sixty-year-olds who are filled with regrets. You hear, "I would have been a physician," or "I could have been a fireman," or "I should have been a teacher." Would have, could have, should have will not make it happen. Lack of purpose, goals, and dreams will create this scenario all the time. I want to make the best of my life, so I refuse to run in circles. I have achieved most if not all of my goals through optimism. Believe in your goals and dreams, that is the first step in achieving them.

Nothing will kill your spirit quicker than an unrealistic goal. I know I will never play in the PGA. That is not pessimism; it is realism. Those who just don't have the voice or have damaged vocal cord will most likely not become professional singers with big followings. Unrealistic goals are a recipe for disappointments, but most goals are achievable with focused dedication to what it takes. Paying off our huge debt may have appeared unrealistic, but we did what it took.

What are your goals? What is your plan to attain them? Maybe you need to make lifestyle changes that will align you with your goal. Maybe you should stop being pessimistic about what you can do. Stay motivated always and celebrate when you reach your short-term goals on your way to your bigger goals. Become consumed with achieving your goals. Live and breathe your goals. Give it your best shot, as I tell my kids. Do not waver in your commitment. I see my daughter continue to make progress in piano because she is giving it her best.

While paying off our debt, I came short of our goals so many times, but with perseverance, I saw it through to the finish. I broke down our debt repayment plans into monthly goals. And I did not get too down on myself when we missed the mark. I kept my wife informed of our progress and in many ways was accountable to her. If you want what you want enough, setbacks will be only temporary. My desire to achieve debt freedom took on a life of its own. The only thing that could have stopped me was divine providence. Trust and do not doubt your goals and dreams; believe me—you will be one step ahead always.

CHAPTER 4

Recognize You Are in Debt

Some of us are at our best when we are boxed in a corner; it has to be a matter of life or death for some of us to fight. Debt became a matter of life or death for me. A cornered animal will fight for its life, but it does not have to be like that when it comes to debt; you do not have to always be in a survival mode. Recognize the implications of the trouble you are in. If you do not understand how you got to where you are in terms of debt, it will be tough to solve the problem.

I never wanted to deal with difficult problems that required me to sacrifice something. I want to live well, but what it was costing me was abhorrent. I was not acknowledging most issues that presented difficulties. I buried my head in the sand regarding our debt, but I soon realized that doing that made our problem fester and grow.

My advice? Deal with your issues. But first, figure out what they are.

Monetary Implications of Being in Debt

I can justify paying off the principal of my debt, but I never got used to paying interest on it. I did not derive any happiness when paying my debts knowing I was only scratching the surface of my principal. Most of my payments went to pay off the interest; in the beginning, there was little to go toward the principal. The debt repayment is structured in such a way that you settled the interest faster than you did the principal. I felt someone was milking me of my money. It was very frustrating and troubling.

To track my debt repayment, I called my bank and got a breakdown of our month-to-month balances. That taught me a lot. I could see how important it was to pay off all the debt to avoid huge interest charges. We had bought our home in 2006, but by 2011, we had barely made a dent in our principal loan amount; I am not kidding! After five years of shelling out money, we had reduced the principal by only 2 percent. We were stuck with this debt, I thought, unless we did something drastic and quickly. The opportunity cost of channeling most of our money toward debt repayment was enormous. To justify not losing too much, for it to make sense to pay off our debt, it had to be done quickly. On the other hand, if we carried most of our debt to term, it will be guaranteed that we would pay every cent of the interest charges. In that situation, you are truly a slave to your creditor. Your creditors will always hope you keep your loan for the full term—in most cases thirty years for a mortgage—rather than pay it off early. They come up with the minimum payment so you can afford it but most important, to ensure they get all the interest they can on the principal loan amount.

I always fought the late-payment charges that were levied when I would miss a payment and got them removed from my bill. The interest charges alone were wreaking financial havoc on us. I thank God I had discipline enough to not miss payments that often.

There are two schools of thought regarding paying off a mortgage. One group discourages paying it off too quickly because of the tax implications. Their argument is that when you pay off your loan, you would not have the interest to deduct from your taxes after that and could find yourself in a higher tax bracket. They believe you will lose in the end.

I belong firmly in the other school of thought that says pay off your loan as soon as you can. This book argues my case. I wondered why those so-called financial experts do not get it. If nothing else, I wanted my peace of mind knowing what was mine was completely mine; I did not want to share my possessions with the bank. It did not feel good handing all my hard-earned money to my creditors. I thought that without the burden of personal debt, I could begin to accumulate enough contingency money. Have you thought about what you can do with money you dole out to the banks? I will leave that to your imagination. I did not want to be a slave to them; I'd rather be taxed at a higher bracket.

As my accountant asked me when I brought up this argument by some not to pay off our loan - if they were so exhilarated about how much they could save with the IRS, why don't they renegotiate for a higher interest rate? That way, they could pay more interest to the bank and have more before-tax deductions in order to ensure being in a lower tax bracket. That reasoning underscored my desire to pursue my debt freedom with immediate alacrity.

The convenience of borrowing from the bank and other financial institutions is unquestionably appealing when you do not have cash to pay off purchases immediately. This is probably one of the reasons people borrow in the first place. Unfortunately, most people do not have a clear-cut plan how they will pay off their debt in a reasonable time.

I have borrowed several times, but on no occasion did anyone discuss the financial implications of what I was about to do. Creditors can sense your need, your desperation and excitement when you come in for a loan. They will not share all the information you need to help you make an informed decision; they would rather not spoil their fun. If they were honest with you, you might not take out a loan with them. They are not about to spill the beans. All they do is snicker behind your back once the loan process is completed.

When I figured out how much I was going to pay in total interest for my house loan, it blew my mind. The bigger the loan, the bigger the interest charges. Duh! It was out of curiosity that I stumbled across a loan interest calculator; I encourage readers to google these.

For the sake of clarity and objectivity, let's consider a $400,000 home loan. An interest calculator is invaluable; it will tell you what banks will not discuss with you. But you deserve to know what you are up against. I plugged in an annual interest rate of 6.5 percent on that $400,000 house with a loan term of thirty years. Can you guess how much you would pay in interest over thirty years for that loan? You might guess $50,000, $100,000, or $200,000 at the high end. My guess would not have been much different from yours!

The calculator produced a different amount. For the life of that thirty-year loan, you would pay a whopping $510,177.95 to be exact in interest alone. Add the principal, $400,000, and it becomes $910,177.95. That is how much you would have paid over those thirty years! Why don't you round it up to a cool million!! Who can come up with that kind of money? How could anyone build any kind of wealth shelling out that much money over thirty years?

Play around with the calculator and see for yourself. Call me the curious cat, but I also researched the word *amortization*, a word often thrown around by the banks when you apply for a loan, but they don't bother explaining it or if they do, you are too desperate and excited to pay attention. "After all it is not a financial class. You only came to borrow," I can hear them say with a snicker.

When you take out a mortgage, the amount you have to pay each month is usually fixed. At the beginning, as you pay your monthly premium, the majority of your payment goes to pay the interest; only a fraction of it goes to reduce the principal. That is why I made payments for five full years and barely made a dent in the principal. Toward the end of, say, a thirty-year mortgage, the majority of your monthly payment would be going toward your principal because less and less would be required to pay the interest on the balance of the loan. This in a nutshell is what I came to understand as amortization. The $510,177.95 is a hidden amount that is never disclosed by the banks but part of the loan if carried to term. How deceitful is that?

This revelation should be a powerful motivation to pay off your loan speedily. It motivated me. We are now able to save a lot of our money by paying off our debt in record time.

If you play with a loan interest calculator, you will see that if you plug in the same total loan amount above and interest rate but increase the amount you pay each month, you will shorten the duration of the loan and end up paying a lot less interest. The term of the loan and potential savings are inversely related regardless of loan amount and or interest rate.

Money saved is money pocketed. You might say that money saved is not physical cash. However, you can pretend to continue paying your mortgage after you have paid it off, but you pay yourself. All of a sudden, you find yourself cleaning up like the banks. You have to be disciplined in order to continue to pay yourself. Isn't that in itself a powerful motivator?

I wanted to keep all my money if I could. I started off with a negative net worth; that is what crippling debt will do to you. I wanted my money to compound over time for my benefit, not for the bank's benefit.

According to my financial advisor, 72 divided by your average rate of return on an investment, let's take 10 percent for example, will equal 7.2; that's the number of years it will take you to double your money invested in a good mutual fund.

To bring this whole point home, the income of an average American family is in the $30,000–$50,000 range. I will take forty as the average number of years an individual will be in the work force, and for the sake of simplicity, we will take $40,000 as the mean income. This means that in forty years, this individual who makes $40,000 can potentially make $1,600,000. Let's say you grab a $300,000 home at 5 percent interest rate over thirty years. You would pay $1,610 per month and $279,767 in interest over the life of the loan. Ultimately, the house will cost you $579,767. But you will also need money for daily living expenses and other things you have to pay, including taxes. Just do the math!

Enough said already. This picture can never be a winner. I choose to be personally responsible and accountable with the money God has mercifully allowed to come my way; I do not want to be the foolish servant who buries his talent. God implores and expects us to use our money wisely. I hope we educate ourselves in financial matters and make sound financial decisions.

Johnson City Rendezvous

When I was accepted into a medical residency training program several years ago in New York, I was excited. The three years I had trained were one of the most rewarding yet tedious periods of my life. I was determined to work hard and complete the training and at the same time live well. I was fulfilling my dream of practicing medicine in the United States and was earning a little more.

New York is very expensive; I had to contend with the high cost of living there. My wife and I had barely enough to take care of our needs, and we found ourselves becoming dependent on our credit cards. We were living above our means but stubbornly refused to acknowledge that. As a consequence, we garnered a lot of credit card debt.

We had more than $30,000 in credit card debt when my wife, son, and I moved to Johnson City, Tennessee, for my first job out of residency. It was supposed to be an exciting time, and I was earning more than I had as a resident.

With more money coming in, we justified trading in our leased car for a new minivan. We owed more on the leased car than we had paid on lease payments, leaving us in an upside-down position. We added that difference to our loan for the new vehicle. As my wife was pregnant, we thought we needed a minivan. To make matters worse, a few months later, I bought a car for myself. At that point, we were about $85,000 in the hole. By the way, we still had that credit card debt. We calculated that we could make the monthly minimum payment, and that was all that mattered at the time. On the surface, it seemed as if we were doing well because we could afford what we had, but at the time, I did not think too much about our total debt.

But after I had a discussion with a financial advisor, I became acutely aware of our debt problem. I called the advisor we used in New York; he had given us good advice in the past, and I believed he had always acted in our best interest. I wanted his thoughts and advice about investing some of our money. He listened but wanted to know more about our financial situation. He could not get past our credit card debt. The advice he gave us was my first real exposure to our debt problem. He told me without mincing words that I had to pay down the credit cards; that was the only way I could free up money to invest. I had to pay more than the minimum or face carrying that debt for years.

I respected that advise and took it seriously. With an honest effort and commitment, we buckled down to address this problem, though initially halfheartedly. We took a deep breath, slowed down our spending, and tackled that debt. It took us two years, but we did pay the $30,000 off. That was one of the hardest, most challenging, but positive financial decisions we had ever made. That was my first rendezvous with focused debt repayment.

What a relief! It felt great to know that we could do that considering the burden we had been carrying. Regardless, we did not sustain that discipline. Though we did not run up our credit cards to that extent again, we did go back to carrying balances.

I began paying more attention to our debt problem but had no real plan to keep us from falling back into debt. The amount we shelled out monthly to pay our car notes took some of the excitement out of paying off our credit cards. It seemed we would never get out of debt. A friend told me that debt was an inevitable part of living in America. I refused to agree with that statement, but with what we went through—being constantly in debt— it sure felt like it was true at the time.

Looking back, our ability to pay off our credit card debt taught me that with commitment and focus, nothing is impossible. That knowledge helped us when we resolved later on to pay off our debt, as we again accumulated much more debt than we could bear. We had worked ourselves into a debt frenzy. We were at that time about $500,000 in debt. You might ask, how could that be? We had thrown caution to the wind; we thought that with more money, we could buy our way to happiness and the American dream. We just hadn't gotten it the first time.

Overcoming Roadblocks to Debt Freedom

I can dream, decide, and wish all I want to, but to achieve my financial goals would require concerted action. James 2:17 tells us that faith without works is dead. Noah could have not believed God and died in flood. He could have let naysayers, negativity, and unbelief distract him from his destiny, but he chose to believe God and build the ark that saved his household and humanity. In like manner, we have to believe our goals and breakdown any barrier that keeps us from reaching them.

Our intention was to get to our goal in a certain time frame. When we set out to become debt free, I was working two jobs at the time. We needed another stream of income if we were to become debt free in four years. I dusted off my rolodex and started calling my friends and other contacts. Within a month, I was working my third job. If I hadn't determined to do that, we probably would still be trudging along in debt today.

I worked all night my first day at my new job. I did not get any kind of rest. I drove home in the morning and fell asleep at the wheel. My phone rang. My loving wife had called me. I woke up on the median between two lanes of the highway. Apparently, while asleep my car had veered off the road on to the median. Thank God I am alive to tell you this amazing story of survival!

That we got to our projected goal was due to more money coming our way. I have procrastinated making those calls and finding that third job. How many times have you sat on a project that had a deadline? What excuses did you give for your procrastination? Are you going to look back ten, twenty years from now and come up with all kinds of could haves, should haves, and would haves? Get on with it already!

If you know what is right but do not do it, you are engaging in self-sabotage. Ironically, I have found myself procrastinating because I feared failure. Defeatist, negative attitudes will always hold us back. I continue to battle such attitudes even as I write this book.

Life is filled with many distractions. I admire the tortoise's focus that let him beat the hare, who let distractions draw his eyes off the finish line. Slow and steady wins the race, but maintaining focus is just as important.

Though TV is an ingenious invention, it is a nemesis to our progress. We can accomplish so much if we do not waste time watching TV; it draws our focus off what's truly important. What are your distractions? You can avoid them if you take time to identify them and use your time better.

The most important roadblock to our financial independence is that space between our ears. It is up to us to think positively and believe we can achieve all of life's promise or dwell in negativity and believe nothing good will come our way. These two belief systems are the difference between winning or losing in life.

I chose to make changes in how I thought about money. I did not bury my head in the sand; I recognized and confronted my shortcomings. I am proud to say that even though the odds were against us, we became debt free because we believed we could.

Good and Bad Debt

Without enough cash flow, you cannot pay off your credit cards every month. That means you have to pay interest on the balance. That is bad debt in that it's avoidable. There is good debt however—debt that can potentially create wealth. Good debt could be money you borrow to get an education or more education, it could also be debt incurred in advertising your business and or buy office space for it, and so on.

Bad debts are liabilities, not wealth generators. In spite of popular belief, mortgages and car loans are bad debt unless you rent out your home or use your car as a taxi to generate wealth. As I look back, I see that the majority of my debts were bad, and I wanted to pay them off as quickly as I could.

Here are the rules: do not carry balances on your credit cards. Do not charge purchases if you cannot pay them off that month. For bigger loans, have a concrete, concise plan to pay them off, and do whatever you can to pay off more than the minimum every month; that will draw down your principal, and you won't pay interest on whatever extra you can apply to your principal. Be conscientious in your debt elimination; you want freedom from debt, not slavery to it.

CHAPTER 5

How We Paid Off Our Debt

It does not take rocket science to recognize a problem. We simply complicate our lives when we ignore what's going on in them. A problem can either be solved or not. Some problems may be attributed to nature, but others we create ourselves. The former we might not be able to change, but the latter is more or less in our hands. Where we came from or the color of our skin is a given, but the amount of debt we rack up is under our control.

Matthew 7:7 tells us, "Ask and it will be given to you; seek and you will find; knock and the door will be opened to you." If I had not been vigilant, I might have remained lost. God knows everything we want even before we ask, but he wants us to open our mouths and request it.

If you can solve your problem, I encourage you to do so. If you cannot, find help—maybe a mentor or coach. Do not work off the top of your head, do not recreate what is already there. There is always a plan; it is up to you to find the best plan for you.

Eureka!

Archimedes was a Greek mathematician, inventor, and physicist who said, "Eureka!" "I found it!" when he discovered a way to detect the amount of alloy mixed with the gold in the crown on the king of Syracuse. I used the same exclamation when I stumbled on a way to eliminate our debt.

As we go through life, we are constantly challenged by one thing or another. If we do not waver but pay close attention, maybe we can learn a thing or two. I try very hard not to be a quitter. Hopelessness can easily create a quitter mentality. I thank God because in my heart of hearts, I believe that good things will come to those who wait patiently. I say this because we humans are an impatient bunch.

I want to preserve and pass on what has worked for me. I remember waiting the better part of two years to get into a residency training program despite decent examination scores. I did not stop applying to accredited programs; I looked at the bigger picture and refused to quit on my dreams of medical training in the United States. It was a competitive process, but it eventually turned out all right.

In like manner, it took several years of waiting to figure out how to pay off our humongous debt. By 2006, we were neck deep in debt because of our mortgage and two new cars as well as smaller debts here and there that all added up. For five years, we were clueless about how to reduce our debt; we just ran in circles and generated more debt.

Even though paying off approximately $500,000 seemed a monumental task, I still believed we could. I told my wife that God had placed this strong belief in my heart that paying off our debt was possible. I clung to that belief for another one or two years.

I was driving home for lunch one day when I heard on the radio about a practical solution to our debt problem. I knew without a doubt that I had stumbled into what I had been looking for. My excitement was palpable; I got home and shared it with my wife immediately. She received it well and encouraged me to look into it. The encouragement I received from my wife was the opposite of what a colleague told me; he said debt was an inevitable fact of life in America. He did not share our vision, so I stopped discussing the matter with him.

A few days after my eureka moment, I received the initial materials I needed to begin this long-awaited journey to debt freedom. I embarked on a year-long financial education and coaching program geared toward better money management, increasing our income stream, and changing our money mentality. The program cost a good chunk of change, but in my mind, anything worth doing is worth doing well. I was not too concerned about the cost; I wanted to be debt free. I found what I'd been looking for all these years and won't give up now.

I came home two or three times a week and took online financial training. I learned how to plug the leaks in our finances, find more ways to increase our money stream, and do away with or tone down activities that made us spend unnecessarily.

The process was not easy; I had to overhaul my spending habits. Previously, I would be home most of my off days, but not any longer. We tracked our spending closely. We embraced the reality of what we needed to do if we were to conquer our bondage to debt. I stayed committed, involved, and passionate and had a great amount of faith in the process. I knew just waving a wand would not eliminate our debt; I knew it would take time considering the amount of debt involved.

Eureka! I found it! If you find something that will make a big, good difference in your life, you do not look back. I encouraged myself every step of the way, and so did my wife and the financial coach I had for a brief period. I knew

I had to surround myself with the right people, and I did. The discovery was worthwhile, but the process was rough!

How We Tackled Our Debt

How did we pay off close to $500,000? It wasn't easy. I knew I needed to be accountable and change my thinking about debt. Staying committed to the process of debt elimination was of utmost importance to me. I realized I could not do it all by myself. But the process I came to embrace did not contain any big surprises.

We came up with a plan to pay off our credit cards, then our car loans, and then our mortgage. I learned to become accountable to other people; that allowed me to remain true and honest with myself and the process. I did not look back. We beat down the distractions that came our way; we recognized the stumbling blocks, dealt with them the best we could, and pressed on toward freedom from debt.

I constructed a timetable for debt reduction and carried it in my wallet for the next three and a half years. It served me well because it kept me in check. I looked at it every so often to remind myself about our intentions as well as gauge our progress. I had to know where we were in order to know where we were going.

I called all our creditors to understand how much we owed, and I signed up with our bank to track our monthly mortgage balance and interest charges. I uncovered all our debt. I did not leave my wife clueless about this; I needed her for support.

I indirectly accounted to our two children by making them aware of our intentions but without all the details. We discussed debt and savings. I wanted to impress on them the importance of commitment to a course of action. They understood we had no quitters in the house.

I began systematically eliminating our debt with money generated by our four income streams. The smaller debts were tackled first using the process I learned. We celebrated every small goal we achieved. We would dance around the coffee table in jubilation with every small accomplishment. We had something to rejoice about, and our successes lifted our spirits. Our kids danced as well when they saw our happiness.

I listened to motivational compact discs over and over to remain charged up and in the present. I kept in mind the importance of never getting ahead of myself. The goals we set for ourselves each step of the way were reasonable and attainable; we took them one month at a time.

We had our fair share of distractions during this process. I came from a large family with many siblings, cousins, nephews, nieces, uncles, and aunts. Things would come up here and there that demanded our attention. We also faced the ups and downs of everyday life. These all came with monetary pressures. Isn't it puzzling how problems seem to come in waves? Most times, a series of problems can knock you down, but our dream of being debt free overshadowed our setbacks and made them temporary. We celebrated our successes one by one regardless of any prior setbacks. We made every effort to avoid extraneous expenses, and we used our money wisely.

There was great excitement in what we were trying to accomplish, but we realized the importance of family vacations to break the monotony; we would come back from them with refreshed and renewed spirits and a passion to get things done.

We paid off our debt using the snowball pattern of debt elimination. Imagine rolling a snowball down a hill and watching it pick up mass along the way. It gets progressively bigger and goes progressively faster. We did this by tackling our small debts first regardless of their interest rates. This is a method postulated by many debt-elimination experts; I cannot take any credit for it. It allows you to see your debts get eliminated one by one, and that gave us great satisfaction. To do this, we paid more than the minimum on our smaller debts until they were gone. While we did this, we made sure to pay at least the minimums on our other debts.

Once one small debt was paid off, we tackled the next smallest debt; we rolled over the amount we had been sending in to pay off the previous smallest debt into the next smallest debt, in addition to paying this next debt's monthly minimum, again, paying above and beyond the monthly minimum. This process went on and on until we achieved debt freedom.

For the sake of clarity, I will objectify this snowball pattern of debt elimination. Let's say that on debt 1, you owe $100, on debt 2, you owe $224, and on debt 3, you owe $636. Regardless of the interest rates on these debts, pay off debt 1 first because it is the smallest, and then you tackle debt 2 and then debt 3. If debt 1 has a minimum monthly payment of $2 (for simplicity's sake, I am not detailing any interest charges), paying it off would take you fifty months. Since you have cleaned out the clutter in your life and have picked up a second or a third job, you can afford to pay $50 toward this debt and pay it off in two months.

You will have paid the monthly minimums on your other debts, but once you eliminate the first debt, you can then start paying that extra $50 on them as well. Let's say your next debt for $224 has a monthly minimum of $4; you start paying $54 a month for that and pay it off in less than five months. Let's say the third debt for $636 has a monthly minimum of $6; you start paying $60 a month for that, and pay that off in less than a year.

In this way, you would have paid off a total of $960 in debt in approximately sixteen months; if you paid the minimum amounts, it would have taken you 106 months! You slashed off ninety months by being faithful and passionate in your debt repayment, and you should rightfully celebrate that!

The more money you put in to accelerate your debt elimination, the faster it will happen. That is the beauty of the snowball pattern of debt elimination. Paying off your debt at a quicker rate means you will pay so much less in finance charges. And I know you have better uses for that money.

At the start, this process seemed overwhelming, but we broke it down into manageable steps. We projected where we would be each month and strived to get there the best we could. We had originally calculated that paying off our debt would take seven years, but I increased our income stream and did so in half the time. Our excitement and passion powered us through the process.

Motivations and results will vary, but the most important thing is never faltering; stick with the process and go at a pace that is manageable but steady. Harness every extra dollar you can lay your hands on. That's exactly what we did.

We sacrificed in the process, but we encouraged ourselves every step of the way. Keep your goal in reach; mine was always in my wallet. Do it the way it works best for you, but always keep your goal in sight.

Be honest with yourself; do not use your credit cards if you have no discipline. Do not be like the alcoholic who thinks that because he has not had a drink in six months he can stop in a bar. Do not tempt yourself; it's not worth it. Literally throw the credit cards away if you do not have self-control.

The word *mortgage* comes from the Latin *mort*, "death," and *gage*, "pledge." The name could not be more appropriate; every debt is like a death grip. I hated paying back money I had squandered, and I particularly hated paying interest on it; I have vowed not to pile up personal debt again.

Debt elimination is possible if you are willing to commit time and money to the process. Be passionate just as I was. The process will stretch you to the limit because it will seem you are pouring most of your extra money down what appears to be a bottomless pit, but you will eventually fill that pit. We achieved debt freedom, but it was a struggle. We failed one time when we were in Johnson City; we'd paid off our debt but fell right back into it.

Here's an analogy: through hard work and effort, overweight people can lose weight, but if they do not change their mind-sets and habits about eating and exercising permanently, they will gain that weight right back. When they can sustain their weight loss over, say, two years, that's an indication they have ceased thinking and acting in the ways that made them gain weight. They understand that maintaining a healthy weight is a process. They cannot look back lest they fall back into temptation. This change in mind-set applies to finances as well.

Could You Benefit from a Coach or Mentor?

Humans are interdependent. God created us to worship Him and to interact and fellowship with one another. If we lived in isolation, I doubt the world would have advanced the way it has over the last two thousand years. We build upon each other and can tear each other down. We do not have to reinvent the wheel. Nothing on earth is actually new; someone has thought of it or done it already. Haven't you thought up a useful gizmo or an idea and then the next day seen it on TV or at a Walmart?

We innately want to do what we want to do. Without guidance and laws, the world would be chaotic. Athletes need coaches the same way students need teachers; the chances of athletes or students succeeding by serendipity is small. As good as Mike Tyson and Michael Jordan were, why did they need coaches? Because they realized the value of coaches.

We all need help to avoid distractions; I can be distracted and fail to live to my full potential. Without a financial coach or mentor, I probably would have run in circles; my lack of discipline would rear its ugly head and prevent me from reaching my goals. We can learn from our mistakes, but we can learn from others how to avoid making them in the first place. We need to be accountable to someone other than ourselves.

My coach directed me to pay attention to areas where we were weak and strengthen them. We were constantly reminded of our goals and was encouraged every step of the way. We were given assignments to educate and increase our knowledge in areas that facilitated our efforts. We were challenged to stay motivated. We needed direction on how to reach our goal. I have never claimed to know everything and as such am always open to learn and grow. The beauty of plugging in with someone who is where you are going is that it makes it easier to get there. All you need is someone who's gone through the process.

I did not have a step-by-step approach toward knocking off our debt, but my coaches did. We paid for their services, but it was worth every penny. We naturally pay for what we value. We became much more organized in our financial matters, particularly our expenses. My wife and I tracked the money we spent on groceries, gas, and our children's extracurricular activities. We tracked our eating out, leisure activities such as golf, and so on. With the knowledge of where our money was going, we were able to plug our monetary leaks. This scrutiny convinced us to cancel a gym membership we never truly used.

We scraped up every penny or dime we could. It was painstaking and tedious, but I began to appreciate the value of cutting down on our expenses and using that "newfound" money to pay off more of our debt faster.

Coaching encouraged me to take on a third and fourth job so we could put more into our debt reduction. In the days before coaching, we simply spent our extra money rather than reduce our debt. The more money we have, the more creative we get with how we spend it. There is always a car upgrade, a high-end watch, and a bigger home beckoning us. We have to change our thinking about the value of extra money; my coaches helped me use ours for good reasons, and the results kept me encouraged.

When we become accountable to someone other than ourselves, we are forced to up our game. I am embarrassed when I do not complete a task my coach or mentor requires of me. It would be unfair to waste my time or my coaches' time through procrastination.

I met with my coach approximately three times a week, and we discussed my progress. I am always expected to give an account of my previous week's endeavors. Accountability was part of why we did very well with the process. We probably would have taken a much longer time to accomplish our goals otherwise; having a coach kept me focused.

I did the same with my overweight patients; I reminded them of their motivation to lose weight and keep it off.

I held them accountable for their actions and gave them encouragement and redirection as needed. Those who stuck with the program did well and were encouraged by their progress and results.

I did not just listen and talk to my coaches; I also read up on financial matters and watched and attended webinars about finances. I lived and breathed the process; I did not miss a beat. This whole process energized me and kept me interested and on the straight and narrow.

I may have made a compelling case about the value of a coach, but having a coach might not necessarily be the best choice for everyone. The very self-motivated could pull it off on their own, but life is about coaching and mentoring.

If a paid coach is not right for you, consider a mentor, an altruistic person with a genuine desire to help others. Your mentor could be your parents, an older friend, a smart businessperson, a teacher, someone at church, and so on.

Shark Tank is a show that combines entrepreneurs and mentors; the former get advice from the latter, who might buy into the business proposal. I watched a twelve-year-old entrepreneur present his clothing business in the hopes he would snag a shark to invest in his business. While he didn't find an investor, one shark offered to mentor him.

A follow up on that story revealed that through the mentoring, the boy had built up his business much quicker than he had anticipated. This underscores the importance of mentorship and coaching—both almost always get you to your goals quicker.

Mentoring is about one person imparting knowledge to another. The mentor has been there and lets the other know how to get there with fewer mistakes and heartaches. Mentoring allows you walk through doors you could not have opened by yourself.

I heard an African-American superstar talk about a free mentoring program that helped boys who didn't have a father or a father figure in their lives. I saw how they pointed these kids in the right direction. This superstar pulled up other responsible men and organized workshops that served these kids' real needs. In this program, they developed a greater appreciation of what it takes to work hard, societal expectations of them, and most important, receive the love they had been deprived of. I saw some of those kids go on to finish high school and get into great universities en route to a bright future. This way of learning is invaluable. You learn hands on. It is practical. Without these sorts of programs, your guess is as good as mine about what the future of these kids would be like.

There is also a theoretical aspect of coaching and mentoring; you can read self-help books such as this one that can inspire and motivate you.

Wherever you find yourself, make the best of your opportunities, keep an open mind, and do not try reinventing the wheel. I will align myself any day with anyone who can keep me on the right track and reduce my chances of making life-changing mistakes. We learn and grow from our mistakes, but I do not want them keeping me from success. If I can get to my goal in one hour, why would I want to spend a whole day doing that?

Parents try to teach and guide their children; they search out their weaknesses and help them strengthen them; it's only natural. Find a coach or a mentor or read a lot in areas you want to improve on. Opportunities do not drop into your lap; your efforts create them. Follow up your dreams by action.

I constantly remind myself that I have not arrived and I want to always do better. I want to remain focused on staying financially independent. I choose to do my part not in a boastful way but through Christ who strengthens me (Philippians 3:17).

CHAPTER 6

Stay Out of Trouble—Be Resolute

When our parents, pastors, and friends tell us to flee from trouble, that's sound advice. If trouble did not abound in our lives, I doubt we would be having any discussion about it. We only have to look around to find trouble. Life would not be what it is if we were not constantly challenged; it would be boring.

We have to be principled and resolute to stay out of trouble. If we allow ourselves to be blown around by the wind in any direction, we will find trouble that can set us back many years. It strengthens us if we manage it well, but at the same time, it can be demoralizing.

I do not drink, but if I constantly go with friends to a bar, chances are I could be tempted by alcohol. On the other hand, if I surround myself with go-getters, their attitude probably would rub off on me. We need to stick with like-minded people or those we look up to. Do not shy away when confronted with trouble, but do not chase it either.

It is okay to say no whenever that is called for. When we are people pleasers, trouble might not be far off. Once beaten, twice shy. I have tasted freedom from personal debt and will do everything in my power through the grace of God to stay out of that trouble.

Debt may not necessarily be your debilitating trouble, but whatever it is you identify as your trouble, deal with it, and if you conquer it, make sure it stays conquered. There is no wisdom in repeatedly falling into the same trouble.

The Struggle to Remain Debt Free

In the last few years, it seemed like every corner I turned, I heard about ways to become debt free. This awareness obviously heightened when we committed to addressing our debt issue. The climax was seeing my church run a program geared toward helping church members find financial peace. It appears to have become a crusade, and I am thankful and blessed to have heeded the call to chase financial freedom against all odds.

What comes after freedom from debt? I consider it a terrible thing to achieve debt freedom but not sustain it. Wouldn't it be sad that after our struggles to free ourselves from debt that we got caught up in that trap again? I was acutely aware of this possibility because I had experienced it. Unless you remain true to yourself and steadfast in your plan, you won't be able to sustain that freedom. The same motivation that helped you accomplish the task should be the same motivation that keeps you out of debt trouble.

It is now more than a year since we achieved debt freedom by paying off our credit cards and car and home loans in their entirety. It is exhilarating to be in this position, but staying there will take talent and character. Your talent will get you where you want to be when your character alone cannot. So many amazing athletes achieve a level of stardom but throw it all away because of lack of character and poor choices; they fall from grace to grass.

Life is not perfect; as you might have gathered from reading this book. Every day, I remind myself to do well. Then, I pay attention to my decisions, choices, attitudes, and actions to make sure they do not contradict my desire to remain debt free. It will continually be a struggle, but I am equal to the challenge through God's grace, and so are you.

Our culture is always chasing new technology. A friend of mine upgrades his smart phone every year, but I think that if something works, there's no reason to replace it. I upgraded my phone after four years of using it, and that was only after it started to malfunction. There is no surer wealth killer than upgrading everything every year.

When everyone around us—neighbors, relatives, and colleagues—is changing cars like underwear, we had vowed to not let that bother us. Our cars are working well; they get us from point A to point B. We take them in for servicing and ignore the suggestions at the dealership that we could do better with newer cars. We'd rather pay for periodic maintenance on our cars than pay notes on new cars for six years. We face a slew of such temptations, but my wife and I thank God for being able to resist them.

We do not worry about keeping up with the Joneses; we want to get ahead financially, so we differentiate between our wants and needs and refuse to be influenced by others. We mentally struggle with this daily, but we overcome it daily as well.

My wife and I monitor our spending and keep each other in the loop regarding our finances. We do not spend arbitrarily. We embrace frugality. These are learned behaviors that we reinforce by constant and open communication. We remind ourselves that we are better off saving money than handing it over to any creditor. We do not buy anything we cannot pay off quickly.

We had equated materialism to happiness and wealth. We were silently showing off. In this material world, it requires a lot of willpower to suppress the desire to spend.

We temporarily put away our cards to reorganize our lives and gain debt freedom; since then, we use them very carefully. We track our spending very carefully and take advantage of the rewards our cards offer us. We make the effort to not carry any balances on our cards, and I suggest that everyone do this.

We are constantly faced with financial challenges because life continues to happen. We cannot stop the eventualities that come our way. After you take care of your debt, you'll be in a much better position to absorb the financial shocks that come your way.

Staying out of debt is the same as keeping weight off—both are lifelong processes that will require hard work, conscientiousness, and discipline. If you keep the weight or debt off one or more years, count that as a job well done. When you can sustain debt freedom, that means you have cracked the code—you now know what it takes.

Be Decisive

Firm decisions need to be backed up by determination. A good decision keeps you on a strong footing because it makes it easy for you to see your direction and goals. If you are wishy-washy, that will forestall your ability to achieve your goals. If you fail to plan, you plan to fail. You have to be disciplined and committed to a course to see any results.

Decisions keep you focused and grounded; they make you accountable to yourself.

We carried our debts for many years because we did not make up our minds about what to do with them, and our indecision negatively impacted our efforts to pay them off. When our credit card balances started going back up, the time it took to pay them off stretched even further into the future. We needed to take a stand.

At times, I thought we were making progress, but I let distractions and other factors derail our progress; I just wasn't resolute enough to cut back on personal spending and make sacrifices; I was not ready to practice self-deprivation. I was still living in the moment and missing the bigger picture. I caved in and we continued to spend indiscriminately.

But I remembered my resolve when I was young to become a doctor. I did not stop until I became one in spite of the difficulties I faced along the way. I refused to waver from my course even if that meant long hours of study and other sacrifices. We only have to look back and find times when we were resolute, determined, and ultimately successful; that can help us face our present challenges.

The difference between pro and amateur golfers is their mental fortitude and their abilities to make the right decisions. A pro golfer's experience and judgment might tell him to stop short of a water hazard when the green is slightly out of reach while an amateur might try to drive his ball over it to the putting green—time and again. My lack of ability to come up with a solid game plan when I play golf results in poor performance. Without my ability to chart a financial course for myself, I would have lost focus and a sense of direction, and I would have fallen short of meeting our goals.

Life can seem complex and confusing especially if our actions are not guided by proper decisions. Many college students today are indecisive and spend more time than they should in college; they switch majors and run up extra tuition bills in the process. Indecision is counterproductive.

I made the decision to pay off our debt. Your decisions will try your patience and require big sacrifices, but you should remain steadfast, so you don't quit in the middle of the game. You'll come out on top as I did. Make the decision first and the other things will align to your advantage. It happened that way for us.

You cannot have your cake and eat it too. Matthew 6:24 states, "No one can serve two masters. Either you hate the one and love the other, or you will be devoted to the one and despise the other. You cannot serve God and money." You have to be committed one way or the other. If you're dissatisfied with your life, you can decide to change it or you can forget about it. There is no time for sitting on the fence.

Stick with Like-Minded People

My mom was the best mother in the world. She was extremely caring, loving, and selfless. She always wanted the best for her children and the people around her. She'd give the blouse off her back to make sure the next person was comfortable. She did not play around when it came to our education. She dedicated most of her adult life to the welfare of her family and provided generously for it. We never lacked moral support when she was around. I interacted more with my mom and gleaned a lot from her. My dad equally was impactful in my life, but for the sake of this brief discussion, I want to concentrate on her.

She wanted me to have good relationships. She treated my friends and classmates with dignity and class when they visited. They always wanted to return because of how hospitable she was. My mom enjoyed my relationships, but she insisted on a good balance. When she noticed I was spending an inordinate amount of time with a date, she showed her dissatisfaction; she didn't want anyone or anything to stand between me and success. She told me there was time for everything.

In hindsight, I see her point; I am a parent who also wants the best for his children. Now I see where she was going with her oversight of me. By her words and actions, she made it clear there were consequences when you mingled with unlike-minded people. It is all good parents' hopes that they lead their children in the right direction; my mom was no different. We know too well that certain relationships can be emotionally and physically consuming. My mom understood the principle of first things first. Having a girlfriend didn't encourage or enable me to pass my exams in medical school.

Sticking with people who do not share in your vision could bring you down quicker than you think. They can explicitly or implicitly antagonize and discourage you. They laugh at your dreams and oppose your progressive spirit. You are filled with regrets because you have allowed them to derail your purpose. Learn to recognize them and keep them at arm's length.

A couple we know needed a sitter; they wanted to go out some days and evenings to keep the flame of romance burning. They had no family nearby, so they were keeping their eyes and ears open at church and at gatherings with friends for a good sitter.

At a friend's party, someone told them about a young woman who was a good sitter in their experience, and she was. She sat for the couple's children and did a marvelous job of it. She was kind but authoritative enough to keep the children in line and safe, and they became fond of her.

The parents came to find out that the teenager was aspiring to become a pediatrician. Her mother told them she was a model and well-rounded student; she was taking college courses while in high school. In addition, she served in church; she made a solid impression on them. They encouraged her every opportunity they had. It was clear the young woman was bound to achieve great things at the rate she was going.

Over a stretch of several months when the couple didn't need a sitter, they did not communicate with her. When they finally reestablished contact with her mom, they were surprised to learn the brilliant young woman they respected greatly was pregnant and near term. She had the baby and within another year and half had her second, all before age twenty. This young woman's prospects and aspirations were jeopardized by early motherhood; she had gotten entangled with an unlike-minded person. She had sadly been derailed and had a very slim chance of achieving her dreams.

Solomon was one of the kings of Israel. The Bible attests that he was endowed with wisdom and to date is regarded as the wisest man ever. The Bible also states that he had seven hundred wives and three hundred mistresses. God warned him to flee from marrying women from other countries and of different faiths, but Solomon disobeyed God, strayed away from him and died foolish.

These are a few examples of how people can be on a worthy course but fall off track because they allow those who do not share in their aspirations and vision into their lives.

It is only natural for like-minded people to hang out together. In school, I tried my best to hang out with other students who desired to do well, and we supported and encouraged one another. There is always a positive outcome with these kinds of interaction. My wife is still my close confidant. I drew support, encouragement, and energy from her as we wiped out our debt. The sky's the limit with like-minded people.

Do you have like-minded people around you? Don't waste any energy on people who aren't rooting for you. Life is rough, and any unnecessary negativity can make it even rougher. More teams win at home because they have their crowds cheering them on. Life is too short; it's all about winning, so cut off the riffraff and start winning.

Position Yourself

Pro golfers talk about positioning a lot. If it is not their position on the leaderboard, it is the position of their golf balls on the fairway—are they in a good or a bad position? Will their position give them an advantage or put them at a disadvantage?

Yes, positioning can be by chance, but largely, people actively seek out advantageous positions. I became a medical doctor because I constantly put myself in the right position to take the next step toward that goal. I burned the midnight oil. I have continued to impress on my children the importance of hard work, which will put them in the right position.

I painstakingly pursued debt freedom because of the advantages I knew I'd enjoy in that position. Being debt free would allow us to open doors that were hitherto closed. When we rid ourselves of debt, it felt like the blinders had come off our eyes. But keep in mind what I said about being debt free; you constantly have to work at it.

Though my financial advisor told me to save up emergency funds, I thought what good would that be if I was still carrying around backbreaking debt? I thought I could accomplish more by paying off my debt as soon as I could. Now, since our debt is out of the way, we can save for emergencies much more easily, and such a safety net is psychologically comforting.

As I mentioned, I watch *Shark Tank*, one of the best shows on TV in my opinion. Self-made millionaires interview entrepreneurs and invest in their ideas and inventions. They can do this because they do not have cash-flow problems. Why should anything stop us from getting into a similar position even if we don't end up millionaires? We should desire to be in positions to take advantages of the opportunities that show up; we cannot do that if we are saddled with debt. At times, I have wanted to invest in a certain stock or another or taken a class. I have enough common sense to know that if you are dealing with debt issues, they can cloud your investment decisions.

Some talk about being in the right place at the right time, but I think Romans 8:28 is more accurate: "All things work together for good to them that love God, to them who are the called according to his purpose." If we find ourselves out of position, God will have our back.

Very uncommonly do things fall into our laps, but it felt that way when I was offered the position as medical director at a nursing home a few years ago. I was not that particularly interested at first, but I mentioned it to my wife, who encouraged me to look into the possibility. After three or so days, I called the administrator. I wondered how they had found me. It turns out that when the place needed a new medical director, they asked around at the hospital I worked and heard good things about me. I eventually took the position and worked as the medical director there for the next couple of years. Most people might attribute that to chance, but I do not see it that way. Hard work pays off because people see it. I believe it was all orchestrated by God. It had everything to do with being conscientious and working hard; everything happens for a reason.

Poor positioning creates doubt and a lack of confidence. I can occasionally shoot a round of golf in the upper seventies (rarely) or low eighties, quite an accomplishment for an amateur. I have found I play the best when my mind isn't cluttered, when I feel confident. That allows me to take shots that leave me in good positions.

Monetary worries can affect our confidence and keep us from positioning ourselves in a way that enables us to help others. Being more charitable becomes easier when you are less burdened by debt. Our charitable acts should not be hindered by our lack of money, but because we are human, they are. However my wife and I have been paying our tithes unencumbered, and we have been doing so for over twelve years.

I was debating where to place this particular point of splurging. I thought it was best suited to be under this subsection on positioning ourselves. Think of it this way— if you are interested in paying off your debt, it doesn't make sense to be extravagant; that will lead to more debt. The enjoyment we derive from extravagant purchases will be dulled and dimmed by our worries about the debt we incur for them. That didn't stop my wife and I from splurging on occasion, particularly after we met a short-term goal, but we learned to do so in moderation.

Go ahead and splurge on occasion, but do it wisely; do not use money you need for milk and bread. You only live once, but you should stay out of financial trouble always.

CHAPTER 7

Be Content but Do Not Settle

Though I work hard, whatever I achieve has been given to me by my Creator; all credit goes to him. Philippians 4:19 tells us, "And my God will meet all your needs according to the riches of his glory in Christ Jesus." Our needs are assured, but in no way does that assurance permit us to wallow in laziness. If we have no need for something, there's no need to pursue it. Discontented people want more than they need.

We have to learn to appreciate what we have. We can begin by giving thanks always. A simple thank you always changes the tone of a conversation. You can do that only if you are truly appreciative. We all want to be happy. I have often run into people before an actual exchange of pleasantries and break out in a wide smile; that almost always elicits the same response. It is an experiment I have tried often enough to say it works like a charm 99.9 percent of the time. People aren't walking around looking for excuses to be malicious. Happiness is infectious; it always lights up rooms and people alike. We need to partake in it often.

Likewise, sharing is a goodwill gesture; it says you want the next person to do well. When we are charitable and pay our 10 percent to our churches, we are demonstrating trust and obedience. These are all virtues that show contentment. We all need to continue to outdo ourselves in these areas of life. Life will definitely be a better place with more of these gestures.

Give Thanks

I'd done many presentations on medical subjects but nothing on what our youth pastor asked me to speak on—thankfulness. It came as a surprise, but it was an honor to be asked. Even though I might not have been the most qualified to speak on that topic, I had a boatload of thankfulness in my heart.

I know I could do better by being more thankful. I can be thankful in my heart, but if I do not express that verbally, it might not carry as much weight. In 1 Samuel 16:7, we read, "For God sees not as man sees, for man looks at the outward appearance, but the LORD looks at the heart." God does not care about our verbal expressions even though there may be a place for that. He searches to see if our heart is right always.

Thank you is an expression of appreciation for a favor or something we have received, but those two simple words are underused and belittled. We all want to be appreciated for what we do, so there is no surer way to win a heart than to express our thankfulness when it is due. Saying thank you is an admission we cannot do it all by ourselves.

Every day I live is a privilege. So much could go wrong, but it goes well many more times. I have had days when all hell broke loose, but I survived them. Nothing is more reassuring when you are imploding than knowing you'll wiggle out of that problem as you did before.

I feel blessed and want to be thankful at all times regardless of my circumstances. It isn't always easy to find those two words in our hearts when going through some stuff. In Philippians 4:6–7, we learn that we are not to feel anxious but in everything, by prayer and supplication with thanksgiving, we are to ask for what we need, and His peace that surpasses all understanding will guide our hearts and minds through Jesus Christ our Lord.

Our debt was a big downer. All I could have done was complain, but that would have killed the can-do mentality we needed to knock off our debt. I can find plenty to complain about, but for good reason, I choose otherwise.

Instead of complaining, we chose to be thankful throughout the process. We could still have been in debt today; I could have lost my job and not have had the money to eradicate our debt. All I needed to do was think about all that could have gone wrong, but because those things did not happen, I am extremely appreciative and thankful to my God for keeping us sane and encouraged.

Every time we complain, we brew up negative emotions that become bad attitudes. If all I did was frown and complain about our debts, that would have created a bad attitude that would have made it difficult to move forward. On the other hand, a thankful heart creates the opposite attitude that propels us to action.

Pride is the reason we are ungrateful. We are not thankful because we take total credit for what we have done and accumulated. Arrogance and discontentment causes us to be unappreciative and unthankful.

When dealing with others, notice how they feel when they are on the receiving end of a thank you. Their faces glow; you can immediately see the appreciation. If everything were perfect, we'd probably have little to be thankful for. I thank God for motivating me to work even harder and be more appreciative. Our debt issue put things in perspective.

You may have heard the saying, "One man's meat is another man's poison." What works well for Nigerians might not necessarily be okay for Americans. A lot can be taken for granted either way, but we have a lot to be thankful for. It takes a lot of maturity to remain humble and subservient. I refused to remain in the status quo, and we thanked ourselves out of debt. We stayed hopeful through it all with thankful hearts.

Hopelessness is tantamount to unbelief; you are simply saying that God won't do what he promised he would do in your life. I do not doubt that God's hand is on my life and my family. I thank him for orchestrating the events that led to our debt freedom. I would never take credit for that. It took a lot from us to do that, and I thank God for giving us the patience and humility we needed.

We all have our fair share of difficulties. We can choose to blame everybody around us or choose to be happy and thankful. Remember these difficult times are what make us tougher; we must be even more thankful in these times.

America sets aside a day in the year for thanksgiving. That is very thoughtful of the founding fathers and helps us keep things in perspective. That does not allow us to wallow in a defeatist attitude or a complaining spirit the rest of the year. The Bible says we should be thankful in everything, and we need to do that honestly and consistently.

Choose Happiness

I am unequivocally happy when my mind is at peace and I am satisfied with my present circumstance. It is our responsibility to find and create our happiness. We cannot wait for others to make us happy—not even our spouses, children, parents, or siblings can do that if we do not allow it. Circumstances and people can affect our happiness, but the burden rests on our shoulders to find it for ourselves.

I play my best golf when I have an uncluttered, happy mind, when I am content. Joy is a deeper feeling of happiness that is not predicated on vain experiences. Joy is always where we want to be; it is the ultimate happiness.

Happiness is circumstantial and usually depends on our situation or what we allow our minds to dwell on; we choose to be happy or not. Optimism is the key that unlocks our happiness. We all want to be happy, but for some reason, we consciously or subconsciously sabotage our happiness by finding everything wrong with our circumstances.

Doubt and negativity are the bedrock of unhappiness. I have caught myself, my wife, and my kids making negative comments on people, issues, and circumstances. One night, we picked up our ten-year-old from an event, and she unleashed her negativity about the evening. "Daddy! The kids there were so unruly. They would not sit in their chairs and were really loud." I believed her; I'd been in the same room with those kids. She was unhappy. I asked, "Do you feel happy or unhappy talking about it?" She admitted not feeling good. I decided to ask her a different question. "What was good in what you did today?" It took her a bit of time to collect her thoughts because she had her mind already disturbed by her own making. She decided to dwell on the negativity around the event, so it took prompting to redirect her. As she began to recount all the good that happened, I saw her countenance shift from disgust to cheer.

Dwelling in negativity produces feelings of unhappiness, whereas positivity always elevates our mood. I deal with negative and positive thoughts daily, but I choose to dwell on thoughts that elate me. Proverbs 23:7 reads, "For as he thinks in his heart, so is he."

I saw eliminating our debt as a positive and holding on to our debt a negative. Any time you pursue something positive, you create happiness. Let go of the negatives; do not let them rule your life; they'll just attract more negativity.

When we consciously embarked on the road to debt freedom, we were headed to a place that offered us peace of mind; we'd be free of the burden of debt, and that thought was one we dwelled on. I was very happy throughout the process because I focused on the right things. Yes there were times when my mind wandered, but one thing I did not allow was to allow myself to wallow in pessimism. These negative thoughts came from nowhere and usually will abruptly stop me in my tracks. It did not feel good at all. My peace of mind was momentarily stolen those times. I did not like it and it was even more motivation to pay off our debt.

We changed our circumstances knowingly and willfully in the same way we created them. I can tell you that after experiencing the humongous burden of debt and the beauty of debt freedom, I will choose all day every day the latter for the happiness it provides. Happiness helps us channel our energy to what is more important in life; any other way is an energy drainer. Sadness steals our energy, makes us mediocre, and kills our momentum.

Every day, I consciously make an effort to dwell on what makes me happy. I have learned that when I disagree or argue with my loving wife over even minor issues, that it saps my energy. My wife acknowledges having the same feelings. Depressed people suffer from low energy; they want to sleep all the time and be recluses. They lose interest in things that they once loved and become underachievers.

Depression is real and, of course, in dire cases requires psychiatric treatment. But refocusing on the positive produces energy and gives us momentum. Debt creates a negative energy. It makes it impossible to fully rise to all

God has called us to be. We can let debt erode our integrity and purpose or do as I did—refuse to continue in that path.

Why are you in debt? Why are you an impulsive buyer? Why don't you see what is wrong? Most people who are in debt got there by looking for happiness in all the wrong places. I remember buying certain items because they made me feel good, but that was only momentary; later on, I felt like hell.

To stay happy, we need to turn around the negativity in our lives and create our own happiness by focusing on all the positives in our lives. We can do that through understanding and desire.

Sharing

Sharing is like giving; it makes others smile. I have seen that happen. Sharing makes other people feel special, especially when they realize you are parting with something special. When you share, you allow another into your space; you give them part of yourself.

Sharing demonstrates selflessness; sharing is a positive act whereas selfishness is a negative act. Whenever we are engaged in positive acts, we ensure our happiness. Sharing is a win-win situation; both parties end up happy campers.

Every time one of our children hoarded a possession, especially when another wanted to play with it, it usually created an unhappy atmosphere. The air was much different when one sibling extended a sharing hand. Adults as well can derive satisfaction from allowing others to know what they know; it shows caring and friendliness.

We can share our knowledge, our time, our possessions, and our lives, and it is nobler when we expect nothing in return. The world would be a better place if we shared more. Homes, neighborhoods, workplaces, and society in general would do better if we shared willingly.

I wrote this book to share what I thought was my compelling story of my journey to financial freedom in the hopes it would benefit others; I did not have an ulterior motive. But several times during this process, I asked my wife why I had gotten myself into writing this book. I had difficulty articulating my thoughts. I had time constraints. I'd read over what I had written and could not even understand myself. A couple of times, I wanted to walk away and just have my peace. But we'd told our kids many times there were no quitters in our house. I could not pass up the opportunity to share something that had changed our lives. My wife and kids would not let me quit; they constantly encouraged me to keep going. They helped motivate me to finish this book.

We turned something that was just a theory about debt reduction into reality, and I wanted to share that. We took a process that was based on a promise and made it come true, and I wanted to share that. If just one person can boast of the same result, my book will have achieved its purpose; that is why I wanted to share my experience.

This book is meant to prove that everything is possible if you dare. Hopelessness is akin to not living. Life is better when we can learn from others or give them something they don't deserve. God's grace is an unmerited love and favor. To live life to the fullest, we must remain very hopeful.

One day during my middle school years in Nigeria, a good friend of mine did a backflip. I was impressed and shocked. I'd seen backflips before, but only in martial arts movies; I'd never seen one live. I felt that if he could do it, I could as well. I begged him to teach me. He was most kind and very happy to teach me to backflip. A few weeks later, I was backflipping! In the same sharing spirit, my son and daughter, as well as some of my nephews, can now backflip because I taught them.

I hope to empower those who are in debt to get out of it by my example, just as my friend taught me to backflip. I hope to embolden readers to dump their pessimism and stir up their optimism. I want to reduce their level of doubt. Others do not have to follow the route my wife and I took; they just have to apply the basic steps, principles, and thought process to achieve the same result; no reason to start from scratch.

Obviously, there has to be an element of trust, motivation, and belief on the part of the recipient in order to do well with a shared subject. Self-help books can give you a rough sketch of a subject matter, but then you have to customize and implement the plan to the best of your ability.

You could pay off another person's debt as an act of kindness, but if that person doesn't change his or her financial habits, he or she would probably end up right back in debt. Imagine sharing with that person something of more value than money to pay off a particular loan—a strategy to become and remain debt free. Give a man a fish and you feed him for a day; teach a man to fish and you feed him for a lifetime.

When people see that something works and not just talks, the chances are they will embrace it, especially if it has the potential of changing their lives. When we set out to pay off our debts, I embraced a coach for a bit, but self-motivation carried me to the finish line.

Sharing fosters companionship whereas selfishness alienates us from friends and can stifle our progress. Selfishness is counterproductive. I am human, so I have been selfish on many occasions. One time, my family and I visited Nigeria when our kids where probably one and a half and three. We brought along a DVD player to keep them entertained. My sister saw it, liked it, and wanted it. I did not give it to her because I thought we had more use for the device than she would. When we came back to America, I do not think we used it at all; it stayed in its case until we ditched it. It was an inexpensive device; we could have given it to her but we did not; we missed an opportunity to be selfless and kind.

Selfishness stems from the mentality of *me me me!* It is a negative mentality that will never foster goodwill. Hoarders pile up stuff because they don't like to share. Our pastor always urges us to open our hands and share; that allows us to receive from God. If we close our hands in an act of selfishness, they won't be open to receive, and we won't have the motivation to share.

Sharing reveals our desire to make the next person better off. We need to share more and not be hoarders. My wife and I have taught our kids the importance of sharing to the extent they do so willingly without much if any prompting.

Be Charitable—Pay Your 10 Percent

God created us in his image; he wants us to act and be more like him. The one thing that makes God God is his insatiable desire to give. One sure way to be like him is to be charitable, which by the way improves our self-worth in that it dispels selfishness. At the same time, it pulls people in need out of their ruts. Act of kindness are signs of obedience to God.

Being charitable gives recipients a reason to be hopeful and puts a smile on the face of the charitable person—it is a win-win situation. There will always be people in need of charity, but that means we have many opportunities to give of ourselves, time, and money.

It is impressive to see people of all walks of life and creeds give of themselves; the effect is far reaching. The promises God has made for those who give are not reserved for just certain people. The act of giving is a catalyst that sets off the promise regardless of who is doing the giving. Part of the reason some have great wealth is their willingness to give.

I would love to be able to give freely and cheerfully. So many situations can potentially rob us of our will and ability to give, and debt is chief among them. But even in debt, we should make a hearty effort to give. So many blessings in our lives are unmerited.

Luke 6:38 says, "Give, and you will receive. Your gift will return to you in full—pressed down, shaken together to make room for more, running over, and poured into your lap. The amount you give will determine the amount you get back." God's promises do not go unfulfilled. Numbers 23:19 tells us, "God is not a man, that He should lie." I believe God.

In a movie, I saw an old woman try to buy ice cream for someone who refused the offer because she felt the giver was on a fixed income, but the woman insisted. She said she would not allow her intended recipient to deny her the blessings and promises that go with giving. The younger woman did not argue with that. For that same reason, I try not to turn down any similar kind gestures that come my way.

America is not squeaky clean, but it's a very giving nation in terms of itself, resources, and money. Leaders give; they don't take. America is respected overseas because of its generosity more than anything else.

But giving can be difficult when you live from hand to mouth. One of my greatest motivations to pay off our debt was regaining the ability to be charitable. It is easier to give when we have an abundance, but we have been instructed to give always even in times of lack. My pastor always says that people should give their way out of poverty and problems.

People are reluctant to give because they are afraid of not having enough for themselves. When they hold on and not give, they directly or indirectly express doubt about God's promises. In Luke 21:1–4, we learn that God cherished the poor widow's mite more than he did the rich, who gave only a little of their net worth.

Our giving (offering) is expected to be above and beyond our tithe, the 10 percent God commanded we give of our earnings. The Bible says that our tithe belongs to God. My wife and I have paid our tithes consistently to our church. Malachi 3:10–11 clarifies God's position on tithing.

> "Bring all the tithes into the storehouse, That there may be food in My house, And try Me now in this," Says the Lord of hosts, "If I will not open for you the windows of heaven And pour out for you such blessing That there will not be room enough to receive it. And I will rebuke the devourer for your sakes."

God was saying that if you pay your 10 percent, he will protect your 90 percent and will bless you beyond your wildest imaginations. "Try Me!" God says in that passage. His word rings clear to me; I will always stand on it.

Our debt freedom is objective evidence of his faithfulness in keeping his promises. We have chosen to obey. I pray that you obey as well by giving and tithing.

Chapter 8

In the Final Analysis

Life is about striking a balance. We have to fulfill our obligations, but we can become overwhelmed if we are not careful. We cannot neglect the various demands on our lives. No one gets a free pass in life; we all need a plan and vision to live and grow by.

We have to cherish what we have and the people in our lives. I love my wife and children; they make life worth it for me. We cannot live and constantly miss the point. Money is good, so make it, but make sure it's a blessing, not a curse. We have to make a good impact on the world around us if we want our lives to count for something.

The Beauty of a Supportive Wife

I could not have asked for a more ideal wife. My wife is God's gift to me. She epitomizes what every man wants in a woman: she's beautiful, smart, loving, kind, patient, and very supportive of me. She is my close confidant.

I met my wife five days after coming to America. We met out of sheer providence. I had accompanied my sister and her family on an outing in Atlanta when I met Dinah purely by chance, it seemed. My little nephew came into the room looking for me; he wanted to introduce a beautiful young woman who was a family friend. He introduced us totally of his own accord. That chance encounter changed our lives.

She and I started talking, and we kept on talking all day. It felt as if we had known each other for years. We really enjoyed each other's company for the next few days until she went home to New York and I returned to New Jersey. Over the next one and half years, we called each other almost daily.

At that time, I was preparing for my foreign medical graduate examination. My examination was as important as making sure that I maintained a healthy communication and relationship with my to-be wife then. I balanced my need to study with my need to nourish my relationship with this wonderful woman. I passed my exam, and I married her.

A good relationship is not distracting; it brings out the best in both parties. She encouraged me throughout the residency application process and has remained an encourager. She has always taken genuine interest in everything that mattered to me. She is my cheerleader, and she creates an environment that allows me to do well always.

My wife and I have agreed on very important issues of our life together such as where we worship, our children's education, where we live and work, and what to do with our finances, but we occasionally have differences of opinion. In such cases, we try to find the middle ground. Though we do not always succeed, we always try.

We moved from Tennessee to North Carolina with high hopes. I wanted us to attend church as a family, but my practice in Tennessee did not allow that. In addition, I wanted to build a traditional primary care practice rather than work in a hospital, as I did in Tennessee. I have never had any issues with my wife concerning my career. She's been completely selfless; she's weighed in on these matters but has always supported me. She's kept me on the straight and narrow and has always given me her best advice concerning work and life situations. She's adorable, and I cherish our companionship.

When we moved to North Carolina, we wanted to buy a home after having rented for five years. I worried whether we could afford the house we liked; the math did not add up for me, but I thank my wife for her strong will. She believed we could afford it. I am more miserly than she is. Buying our house was a great accomplishment, but it provoked my anxiety. When it came to cutting back and making the necessary lifestyle adjustments necessary to free ourselves of debt, my wife jumped in headfirst; that is my kind of woman---gracious!

Wealth

Most people use the word *wealthy* to describe people with many material possessions. I used to think wealth should be flaunted; if it isn't, it's not there. Of course, that is not necessarily true.

A good friend of mine was on staff at a historically black college in the area. He was invited to a meeting one of the school's major donors attended. This very generous man gave millions to the school every year, but he was unassuming and down to earth—no flashy attire or big rings that suggested affluence.

When the donor left, my friend decided to see what kind of car he drove. He peeped out the window and saw the wealthy man drive off in a ten-year-old jalopy. That was not his vision of this supposedly affluent man.

Wealth has also been associated with certain professions—physicians, engineers, lawyers, pilots are usually assumed to be rich. However, it's rare that people consider the liabilities the wealthy have taken on; they just marvel at their mansions, planes, fleets of cars, and so on. By flaunting their possessions, the wealthy are vicariously telling us how wealth should be perceived. The media has a hand in what we perceive as wealth today. It is a ploy to brainwash others.

If wealth is all about material possessions, why can't some sustain them? Circumstances beyond our control can threaten our wealth, but so can living beyond our means. All that glitters is not gold. We have to calculate the value of something objectively; it could be a liability rather than an asset.

I lived for twenty-eight years in Nigeria and more than fourteen in the United States. Here in the States, we rely heavily on credit, while in Nigeria, cash is king. The concept of wealth in Nigeria is different from what it is in the States. Families there who can afford three meals a day, a power generator to handle power outages, a car, and a consistent water supply are considered wealthy; almost all Americans would be perceived as wealthy by Nigerian standards. How much we take for granted in America!

And even in Nigeria, as a resident of a city, my perception of wealth was different from the one those in villages had. There, wealth is measured in terms of the land you own. People can have different definitions or perceptions of wealth, but generally, it is associated with material possessions. In reality, wealth consists of so much more than just material possessions; what you have saved increases it, while what you owe decreases it.

Most people understand the purchasing power of money and its power to solve problems, but too many chase wealth so they can flaunt it and satisfy their desire to be envied. They might be technically wealthy measured in terms of material possessions, but they could be poor in terms of their debt. I know because I have been there. Nonetheless, they never feel satisfied, and that drives them to buy more and go deeper into debt.

During my years of residency, I contributed to a retirement plan; one of my brothers who was in such a plan had enlightened me. I was told that I'd be tempted to spend the money otherwise. Whatever I put automatically into a retirement account would grow over the years as I put more in and earned interest on all of it. I believed my big brother and contributed to my account.

I began hearing about the concept of net worth much later, after I decided to rid myself of debt. I became much more aware of the financial terminology when my interest in the matter debt freedom was heightened.

Net worth is the amount of our assets minus our liabilities. The first time my wife and I calculated our net worth, I was shocked to learn we were in the red—we had a negative net worth. We owed more than we owned in spite of the fact we had accumulated many material possessions.

Knowing what our net worth was, we were eager to change the situation. Over the next several years of paying down our debt, we saw our net worth go from red to green, from a negative to a positive figure, and it's been that way ever since. I stumbled upon a great app for my smartphone that tracks our net worth effortlessly. We plugged in our assets and liabilities, and it updates our finances, accurately showing our net worth; it's so much less cumbersome than the Excel spreadsheet I had used. I have seen other apps that serve a similar purpose, and most of them are free.

Just as my overweight patients have to step on the scale regularly to check their progress, we were able to check out our financial progress at any time. I encourage you to start tracking yours. You will never know where you are going if you do not know where you are at any one moment. You will appreciate your progress when you start tracking it.

The Millionaire Next Door by Stanley and Danko is one of my favorite books; one of my coaches told me to read it. It talked about how to appropriately deduce your net worth by a simple calculation. This excerpt will elucidate this point.

> Whatever your age, whatever your income, how much should you be worth right now? From years of surveying various high income/high net worth people, we have developed several multi variate-based wealth equation. A simple rule of thumb, however, is more than adequate in computing one's expected net worth.

> Multiply your age times your realized pretax annual household income from all sources except inheritances. Divide by ten. This, less any inherited wealth, is what your net worth should be.

> For example, if Mr Anthony Duncan 41 years old, makes $143,000 a year and has investments that return another $12,000, he would multiply $155,000 by 41. That equals $6,355,500. Dividing by ten, his net worth should be $635,500. (*The Millionaire Next Door*, 13).

The book broke down this expected net worth/wealth more, and here's where it gets even more interesting.

> Given your age and income, how does your net worth match up? Where do you stand along the wealth continuum? If you are in the top quartile for wealth accumulation, you are a PAW or prodigious accumulator of wealth. If you are in the bottom quartile, you are

a UAW, or under accumulator of wealth. Are you a PAW, or UAW or just an AAW(average accumulator of wealth) … To be well positioned in the PAW category you should be worth twice the level of wealth expected. In other words, Mr Duncan's net worth/ wealth should be approximately twice the expected value or more for his income/ age cohort, or $635,500 multiplied by 2 equals $1,271,000. If Mr Duncan's net worth is approximately $1.27 million or more, he is a prodigious accumulator of wealth. Conversely, what if his level of wealth is one-half or less than expected for all those in his income/age category? Mr Duncan would be classified as a UAW if his level of wealth were $317,750 or less (or one-half of $635,500). (*The Millionaire Next Door*, 14)

I have applied this formula to our finances, and I suggest you do the same. The book was really an eye-opener. I recommend it to anybody who wishes to learn more about the characteristics of American millionaires and most important the behavior and mentality that will allow you keep your wealth, in turn increase your expected net worth at any income level.

Contentment and True Wealth

Our true wealth is our interpretation of what wealth really means in our lives. What produces a sense of contentment in you regardless of how rich you are? We are content when we can appreciate any situation we find ourselves in. I have seen people with many material possessions but little contentment with their situation; they always want more.

If we can be content in whatever situation we are in, we are close to achieving true wealth. I do not have five laptops and six cars; just one of each suits me just fine. When I was growing up, I had to live within my means; I did not have a choice. Money was tight, and of course I didn't have any credit cards. I was always tempted to possess more and more but fortunately, I couldn't. I had what I needed any one moment.

I'm the eleventh of eighteen children, and I looked up to my older brothers and sisters. I never felt a compulsion to jump the queue to get to where they were at any one time. I was in medical school when most of my older siblings where already established in their professions. Before I completed medical school, most of them were already married and had one or more kids; six of them lived in the United States then.

There was never a dull moment whenever we got together; we had fun! It was incredible that I remained focused enough and knew my situation was only temporary. I was content and knew the importance of making the best of my situation then and not acting stupidly. Contentment is a temporary place; when you are content, you continue to work hard to reach the next level, where your contentment is demanded again for a period.

Contentment has to be conscious and intentional. Even though I lived with my brother and his family for free when I came to America, I still found ways to generate debt. I was far from content. I gave in to my desires; I was foolishly excited. I wasn't thinking about the trap that debt represented.

It takes exceptional discipline to live within our means nowadays; there are so many temptations to spend our money. In residency, I made a decent income, enough to live well on, but I nonetheless spent foolishly and ended up in debt. I lived paycheck to paycheck. I was never content; I constantly overreached and wanted more.

Material wealth doesn't guarantee happiness. You can be wealthy, but if you do not focus on what really matters—God, family, and friends—you will never learn the meaning of true wealth. For me, true wealth is understanding how to balance work and life in a way that allows you to be kind and charitable without the worries of debt. True wealth is about sharing and giving, not living in bondage.

Have you ever given freely with no regrets or misgivings but in a good spirit? It feels really good to give when I do. Giving changes the dynamics of wealth. At that point, you can acknowledge that your financial blessings are meant to bless others. No wonder people like Oprah and Bill

Gates and other altruistic people replenish and even grow their wealth by their continual giving. Stingy people bring scarcity upon themselves. I've found myself many times acting in a stingy manner and other times giving freely, and I definitely love the feeling I get from giving freely. God gloated about giving his only begotten son.

Debt is greed manifest; it represents selfishness. Living on borrowed money enslaves you; being debt free leaves you with little room to make excuses why you cannot give.

Find joy because that is synonymous with true wealth. When we find joy, nothing should shake us up. Share and give. There is no joy in material wealth if all we do is hoard it for ourselves.

CONCLUSION

Life is too short. Whatever you want to do, do it quickly because before you know it, your life will be over. When we take vacations, time flies by and we wonder where it went. We give up easily and too quickly. Time has been given to us generously and it is valuable; if we manage it well, it can solve most of our problems, but it can never be made up once it slips by.

I have started but not finished projects because I can manufacture excuses at the drop of a dime. Those times when I buckled down, however, I did well. I always wanted to play piano, so when our children were taking lessons, so did I. I had tried that before but had given it up. However, I was determined to stick with it this time. I told myself that fifteen to thirty minutes a day of practice was doable. I was enthused getting back to it, but my passion began to wane because I caved into the hustle and bustle of life once again. Unfortunately, we allow so many factors to keep us from achieving our goals and many times refuse to acknowledge them. We often abandon our projects because they aren't do-or-die situations. It could be that we are not committed enough.

But look at your accomplishments and learn a thing or two from them. Whenever you achieve something, that's due to the passion you put into it. Borrow a page from your past accomplishments to see you through to your next accomplishment.

As parents we instill in our children the importance of loving what they do and the need to complete what they start. Anything worth doing is worth doing well. Our kids achieved black belts in karate due to their drive and ambition to do so.

But too many activities can produce chaos when we really need order; that explains why we can drop out of a project and sabotage its intended outcome. We must strive for a balanced lifestyle.

Think things through. Do not start something because your neighbor is doing it; start something because you intend to finish it. When we started freeing ourselves of our debt, we could have given up if we had listened to the naysayers. The odds were against us, but our desire and passion saw us through to our goal; it would have been impossible for anyone to stop us.

Where is your life force? What motivates you to keep going? Let whatever it is always be in the forefront of your life; forget the Joneses. We're all equipped to run this race of life or we would not be here. Let truth and honesty rule and guide you every step of the way. If we had buried our head in the sand about our debt, I probably would not have written this book.

Impulse spending is a wealth killer. Be conscious at all times when you spend your money. Don't go into a store for one item and come out with six. If you feel you need more material things to be happy, you have an obvious void that only God can fill. My God is in control. He is real.

We innately desire to do well but can become our own saboteurs. I have come across opportunities but shied away from them. A promising NBA player was on his way to outdoing himself. During an all-star game, another legendary player told him how much he admired his talents and that he would bring his children to watch him one day; that showed this young man's talent and star qualities. But then I watched this young man's career go from good to bad; he ended up being traded all over the place. He never reached his full potential. I hope and pray we all reach our God-given potential.

What does not kill you will strengthen you. We'll all face tough times, but if we're tougher, we'll outlast them rather than give into pressure and quit. My debt was a financial stressor, a real downer. Our children come under fire when they misbehave at home or in school; they are punished accordingly. Every action has its consequences. They are learning every day that good behavior attracts good consequences just as bad behavior attracts bad consequences.

Pressures and temptations are bound to happen, and if we do not faint, they might well be stepping stones to success. We may wish problems never come, but I can assure you that if it were not the case, we'd never know how to appreciate anything good.

> No temptation has overtaken you except what is common to mankind. And God is faithful; he will not let you be tempted beyond what you can bear. But when you are tempted, he will also provide a way out so that you can endure it. (1 Corinthians 10:13)

What a powerful reassurance from our God to us.

People do not like taking responsibility. At times, I have blamed others for my misfortunes, but that never goes well; I do not come out better off. Being responsible requires maturity and an understanding that the burden is on us to make the situation right. I blamed the system and our circumstances for the reason we got into debt; I now realize it was our fault. If I had clung to that culture of irresponsibility, we would never have gotten out from under our crippling debt. We have always encouraged our kids to own up to their mistakes. When they say, "He or she made me do it!" I ask if they were dragged or forced into that problem. Their consistent response? "No."

There is value in learning from other people's mistakes; apprenticing ourselves to a coach or mentor cuts down on the time it takes us to learn something and reduces our chances of making lifelong mistakes. Matthew 14:14 tells us that if a blind man leads another blind man, they will both fall into a ditch. Be mindful of who you are copying or following. Find someone who has been where you want to go—that's the value of a mentor.

We owe it to ourselves to be happy; the opposite emotion is bad for our health and our lives. I know worrying does not solve any problems, but I constantly find myself doing so. It is a big prayer of mine to reduce my inclination to worry. Worrying creates a negative air around you and keeps you from accomplishing your goals. Most of what we worry about never happens, so why bother worrying? Where there is doubt, you'll find failure.

It's okay to live life to the fullest. Yes, money matters and definitely makes life easy, and hard work never kills anyone. But first things first; make a great effort to love God, your family, and your friends; that leads to a contented life no matter how much wealth you accumulate. Surround yourself with people who encourage you. I rest assured that God is not man that he should lie (Numbers 23:13). The sky's the limit when you trust him and do right. Find the right people and the right mentality and get on your way to debt freedom. You can do this. We did. I wish you the best in all your endeavors.